CONSTRUCTING
&
CALCULATING
BOND INDICES

A Guide to the EFFAS Standardized Rules

Patrick J. Brown

Probus Publishing Company

Cambridge, England
Chicago, Illinois

Designed, illustrated and typeset by Nick Battley, London, England

ISBN 1 55738 814 8

Printed in Great Britain at the University Press, Cambridge

Contents

Cont.

(cont.)

Cont.

(cont.)

Cont.

(cont.)

Foreword

by the Chairman of the EFFAS-European Bond Commission

"Calculating a new index is simple!", explained a young analyst to me just a few days ago. I remembered that I had held the same opinion some ten years ago, as I embarked on the construction of my very first index. But, as is so often the case, those things which initially appear simple invariably turn out to be incredibly complex. As I have learned to my cost, this adage holds especially true for index construction. Furthermore, while the development and calculation of any new index is complex enough, the construction of an index which *truly* reflects the development of a certain capital market segment is quite another matter.

At the beginning of the 1980s, the EFFAS-European Bond Commission (EFFAS-EBC) began development of a bond index family which has since become known as the EFFAS bond indices. The main aim of this index family was the creation government bond indices for most European countries, each calculated on the basis of a common methodology. After almost ten years of operation, however, it became clear that the original construction and calculation methods were no longer appropriate to deal with the many developments in the markets which had taken place during that period.

A sub-committee of EFFAS-EBC was set up which, together with representatives of most international bond index suppliers, held lengthy and thorough discussions on a blueprint for modern bond index calculations. The result of this activity was the production of a broad range of rules for bond index construction and calculation, which reflect both the wide variety of global fixed-income instruments and the different benchmark needs of today's portfolio managers. In turn, these rules have enabled a new generation of EFFAS indices to be born and they have created both a reason and a purpose for this book.

Pat Brown, an internationally-renowned expert in financial mathematics and indices, has undertaken the difficult and time-consuming task of collating and assessing the output of the numerous meetings of the EFFAS-EBC sub-committee, and has structured and refined the many drafts of the rules for the EFFAS Bond Index. Fortunately, for the financial community at large, Pat soon recognized the need for this publication and he has combined the results of the sub-committee's deliberations together with his own personal, and profound, knowledge of the subject to produce a book which not only provides full details of the EFFAS rules and recommendations but, importantly, discusses the rationale behind them.

In these times of rapidly growing cross-border bond trading and investment, indices are becoming increasingly important not only as instruments for the true and fair evaluation of whole sectors and markets, but as investment products in their own right. Since they serve as an accurate means of measurement of market performance and as benchmarks for comparison of their component issues, their growing importance as capital market instruments is underlined by their increasing use as underlying assets for futures and options contracts.

Therefore, it is my belief that this book—to the best of my knowledge unique in its field—will soon become the standard work for bond index constructors world-wide.

Vienna, March 1994

Peter Schedling

Preface

by the Chief Executive and Secretary General of ISMA

In recent years there has been an increasing globalization of the world's capital markets as evidenced by the huge increase in turnover in cross-border trading. As a true global market emerges and institutional funds can switch relatively smoothly from 'domestic' to 'international' and vice versa, this trend can be expected to continue. The swaps and derivatives markets are now so closely correlated to the cash market that an invisible thread effectively connects them in many products and currencies. The dissemination of information and data really has reduced the financial industry to a global village.

With the globalization of the markets has come the need for standardization of financial data for comparative purposes.

ISMA, as the market regulator for the world's largest free capital market, fully supports the aim of EFFAS-EBC in standardizing the construction and calculation of bond indices. We regard this as an essential element in the assessment of value in markets and market sectors, by facilitating their comparison and thereby promoting increased liquidity to the advantage of all.

I am particularly pleased, therefore, that this process has now been completed and that Pat Brown of ISMA has set down the agreed standards in what I feel sure will become the definitive work on the construction of bond indices.

Zurich, March 1994   *John L. Langton*

TOTAL ACCESS
TO THE BOND MARKETS

Bloomberg Financial Markets provides up-to-the-minute global financial news, complete bond market data and analysis on-line through THE BLOOMBERG. Through unique functions including EFFAS Indices, Bond Switch, Searching Functions, and Portfolio Management Systems, BLOOMBERG delivers the crucial information and analysis to help you maintain a competitive edge.

Bloomberg
FINANCIAL MARKETS
COMMODITIES
NEWS

The Next Generation of Financial Intelligence

Chapter 1

Introduction

In the early 1980s, it was found that there was no satisfactory portfolio performance yardstick that enabled one to compare individual bond markets on a day-to-day basis. The European Federation of Financial Analysts Societies (EFFAS) Commission on Bonds[1] felt that these needs should be addressed and consistent solutions found. As a result, a joint approach to the problem was agreed and the Datastream/EFFAS bond indices were born.

It was felt that the government bonds in each domestic market normally form an active homogeneous market which can be compared with other markets. Therefore, these were the first to be calculated. Each domestic bond commission was asked to select all those bonds which it felt constituted comparable government bonds. Initially, the mandate appeared simple. However, at that time, such was the diversity of market structures, instrument types and market practices, that the authors had considerable difficulties in achieving standardization. In the end, a number of compromises had to be made. These covered a wide range of problems. For example, the German commission had difficulties with the start date for including new bonds, that is, not the first trading date, but the official date—which could be up to 6 months later; the French maintained that BTANs[2] were not bonds, but money market instruments. With many markets comprising instruments with various structures such as serial bonds in the Netherlands, stepped-coupons (both up and down) in Belgium, extendible bonds in Sweden, floating-rate bonds indexed on Treasury bills in France and floating-rate Treasury bills in Italy, selecting those bonds which

---

[1] *The EFFAS-European Bond Commission (EBC) was originally set up in 1976 as a Standing Commission of the European Federation of Financial Analysts Societies to cover bonds. The EBC, which draws on the domestic Bond Commissions of the member countries, comprises the leading bond experts within each country. Members include heads of research, analysts, economists, investors, regulators, futures & options experts. Meeting four times a year, the Commission's goals are: 1) to raise the standard of bond analysis across Europe; 2) to help to standardize practices across Europe (e.g. in areas such as yield calculation, bond indices, instrument features); 3) to provide information on the European bond markets to enable people to participate with confidence.*

[2] *BTANs are now treated as bonds, and are to be included in the CNO indices.*

enabled comparability was a hard task. As expected, the numbers of bonds varied greatly from country to country.

The indices initially covered the government bond markets for Austria, Belgium, Denmark, Eire, France, Germany, Holland, Italy, Norway, Spain, Sweden, Switzerland and the United Kingdom. Soon afterwards, indices were added for Japan and the United States. It was the original intention that the same methodology should then be used for indices covering different market sectors and markets; however, with the exception of the eurobond market, the methodology was not extended.

Having selected these bonds, it was recognized that the maturity structure of each market varied dramatically. Despite this, however, it was obvious that a number of sets of indices should be calculated for most markets. These were:

- All bonds with a life of at least 1 year

- Bonds with a life of 1-3 years

- Bonds with a life of 1-5 years

- Bonds with a life of over 5 years

The selection of the two subsets, 1-3 years and 1-5 years, allowed for the most common investment ranges in Europe, although there was quite a variance from country to country. Bonds under 1 year were excluded because it was felt that they were either treated as money market instruments or were illiquid.

Around the same time, the International Securities Market Association (ISMA) (then the Association of International Bond Dealers (AIBD)) started calculating indices for straight eurobonds using the same methodology. The eurobond indices were calculated for all large (not just government) issues in US dollars, Australian dollars, Canadian dollars, euroguilders, European currency units, Japanese yen, sterling, Deutschemarks and Swiss francs. Of these only the US dollar section was subdivided into maturity time bands.

Later, several organizations (including J.P. Morgan, Salomon Brothers, Paribas and Lehman Brothers) started publishing bond market indices; these, however used different formulae and selective criteria and so were not strictly comparable.

In 1990, it was noticed that the Dutch Datastream/EFFAS indices had performed differently to other indices, and had proved very difficult to outperform. As a result, a paper was produced by members of the Dutch bond commission (see Bibliography), which highlighted a number of particular points[1]. As a result, the EFFAS/European Bond Commission felt it right to re-examine the basic rules for bond index construction and try to derive universal guidelines in order to standardize the methodology. The sub-committee was widened to include not only the members of the European Bond Commission, but also representatives from the UK Institute of Actuaries, the French Comité de Normalisation Obligataire (CNO), various international institutions who calculate bond indices (such as J.P. Morgan, Salomon Brothers, Lehman Brothers, Merrill Lynch, Paribas and Datastream) and ISMA. By drawing on this wide range of expertise—which covered all the domestic and international bond markets—it was hoped that a standardized methodology could be determined, similar to the ISMA (AIBD) formula for yields, so as to allow true comparison of indices and replication.

It was decided that the terms of reference of the index sub-committee should be:

- To discuss and examine all aspects of the construction of international bond indices;

- To derive a set of rules for the construction of international bond indices, together with any associated calculations;

- To publish the results.

Datastream was asked whether they would like to develop the new indices. Sadly, due to internal difficulties at that time, Datastream informed the EBC that they would be unable to provide the resources required to both develop and produce the new indices. As a result, Bloomberg LP were approached and they agreed to provide the necessary support for the project.

Meetings were held monthly throughout Europe during the basic discussion and review process. Once the basic rules were determined, and following a top-down examination, the whole set was re-examined to remove any internal inconsistencies. The formulae were then produced. A series of weekly meetings were held to iron out remaining inconsistencies and other minor deficiencies and it was at this point that some rules were found not

---

[1] *It transpired that the different results were caused by the treatment of serial redemption bonds and the move by the Dutch government to issue bullet bonds. The Datastream/EFFAS indices included both serial and bullet bonds, whereas the J.P. Morgan and Salomon Brothers indices only included bullet bonds. Since during the period being compared yields were rising, bullets were underperforming serial bonds with their earlier redemptions. As a result, the Datastream/EFFAS indices outperformed the others.*

to be practical in certain countries and were therefore re-evaluated. Work then started on producing the new Bloomberg/EFFAS bond indices and the ISMA eurobond indices. The construction of the indices necessitated a few minor adaptations. Finally, as these indices appeared, each was carefully examined to find out whether further refinement was required.

Given such a diversity of securities, market conventions and practices as presented by the world bond markets, we believe this period of almost destructive testing was essential to remove all the 'bugs'. The sub-committee believes that the rules described in the following pages are as 'complete' as possible. However, since bond markets are continuously evolving, there can be no doubt that further refinements will be required.

The aim of this publication is to place the ideas and rules for global bond indices in the public domain. In this way, users of indices can fully comprehend how they are constructed, the biases which are introduced, the extent and limitations of the calculations and, finally, the comparability of different indices. Fund managers, who are using the indices for performance measurement, need to know the nature of the indices in order to select the index to outperform. They also need a transparent index with daily output. Furthermore, the indices should also be available in a form that allows such users to create their own customized indices to reflect their own needs. This can be done by combining these indices according to the formulae given later.

The sub-committee would like to thank all their members for their unstinting efforts, their companies for allowing them to share their expertise and for granting the time and facilities to complete this work. We would also like to thank the EFFAS/EBC members, Bloomberg and ISMA for their hard work in bringing theory to practical conclusion.

Chapter 2

Purpose and basic principles

It was felt that the main purposes of these indices should be:

- To act as a benchmark for portfolio management;

- To act as an indicator of market performance and development. This should include price and yield performance, as well as structural information, e.g. average maturity, duration, convexity, etc.;

- The basis on which market options & futures may be derived;

- A comparator for different markets.

Many of the current indices have evolved over time and are restricted to the domestic government and eurobond markets. Since the original point was often based on that institution's database, usually supporting its own trading in different markets, the underlying structure varied dramatically. The indices employ differing formulae, variations in bond selection, construction methods and price derivation. In addition, many of these indices are *not* transparent, in that the constituent bonds or the methodology for selecting them at any one time are not published. Further, there is a need for greater segmentation in relation to the life expectancy of the constituents, the type of issuer, the type of security and other selection criteria. This would allow users to 'reconstruct' indices that were more realistic to their needs. As a result new composite indices could be created which more closely match the portfolio manager's constraints and weightings.

It was also felt that any recommended calculations should abide by the following basic principles:

- The indices should reflect the experience of the average holder in the sector;

- The calculations should be reproducible by another party;

- As far as possible objective, rather than subjective, criteria should be used in selecting and processing the data;

- The criteria used for selecting the securities and the source of the data used should be published;

- The formulae used should be published;

- The performance of an index should reflect the percentage change of the market over the relevant time period, i.e. it should be independent of the base date;

- The calculations should only be based on data relating to the constituents. An example of this is in a standard redemption yield calculation, where the assumed reinvestment rate for coupons is that for the bond itself;

- The calculations must reflect changes in the structure of the market in a timely manner (e.g. it must allow for new issues, redemptions etc.);

- The calculations should be applicable to a wide range of bond markets and sectors of markets. The markets may be, for example, subdivided according to type of borrower (e.g. governments, government agencies, corporates, banks and supranationals) or life expectancy of the issues;

- It should be possible to calculate specific indices using the same methodology which can be compared with the published indices;

- The indices should reflect the performance of a portfolio which contains the same specific percentage of each of the securities in the index. Whenever any cashflow occurs, this is absorbed in or removed from the portfolio and the portfolio is assumed to be re-balanced across the possibly revised constituents without any cost;

- The indices must be valid over a reasonably long time-horizon, i.e. over several years.

Some of these principles can, in fact, be derived from others. For example, the requirement for any index calculations to be reproducible by another party implies that the selection criteria must be objective and the formulae published.

In practice it will be seen that although the proposed calculations comply with the above principles, it is unlikely that two organizations calculating the same index between the same two dates will end up with identical calculations—even if they start and end with identical prices—since the intermediate values can affect the results[1].

[1] For two organizations to calculate identical total return indices, the combined market value of the constituents must be identical whenever a coupon is paid or the constituents change in any way. The resulting differences should not be significant.

Is your International Securities Data coming from the right source?

In an uncertain world, there's only one place to get your data. Straight from the horse's mouth.

As the official body in the market the International Securities Market Association has more data, more easily available than anyone. Our complete database includes daily updates on 7000 prices, the latest Eurobond issues including European domestic government bonds, historic prices and up to 200 fields of information on individual bonds. All accessible in printed or electronic form. No wonder we're the market's most sought after resource when it comes to international securities data.

Why horse around?

For further information send a copy of this advertisement and your business card to:
International Securities Market Association Ltd., Seven Limeharbour, London E14 9NQ.
Fax (44-71) 538 9183. Or call (44-71) 538 5656.

I S M A

Chapter 3

Index methodology

This chapter describes some of the discussions, compromises and the conclusions arrived at in trying to create an objective set of rules for the construction of international indices that comply with the purposes and basic principles that have been outlined.

Portfolio emulation

It is essential that any index calculation should emulate the nature and performance of a portfolio.

A portfolio consists of a number of holdings of different sizes by value. It was felt that if a portfolio manager holds the same percentage of all the bonds in the index then his performance should be identical to that of the index. Conversely, any deviation from these average holding percentages should be reflected in his performance above or below the index.

»Example

Consider an index which consists of two securities A and B. A has a value of US$ 1m, while B has a value of US$ 10m. Let us assume that our portfolio holds 50 per cent of both securities, then its portfolio value is:

$500,000 + 5,000,000 = US\$ 5,500,000$

- *Scenario 1*

If the price of A halves and the price of B doubles, then the value of the portfolio becomes:

$\frac{1}{2} \times 500,000 + 2 \times 5,000,000 = US\$ 10,250,000$

- *Scenario 2*

On the other hand, if the price of A doubles and the price of B halves, the portfolio becomes worth:

$2 \times 500,000 + \frac{1}{2} \times 5,000,000 = US\$ 3,500,000$

Hence, the performance index should be weighted by the size of the holdings.

Some stock market indices (e.g. the UK Financial Times 30 and the US Dow Jones Industrial Average) do not weight the constituents of the index by their size, but multiply their prices together to derive the index. Thus, they do not reflect the performance of the total market portfolio.

In the example above, the index would remain unchanged for both price scenarios, as the price of A times the price of B is unchanged. This approach is obviously unsatisfactory at emulating the performance of a portfolio, although it does give a reasonable indication of short-term price movements. Such calculations are called 'geometric index' calculations. They are discussed in more detail in Appendix A.

It is felt that, ignoring the presence of any cashflows, if the total value of the underlying investments in an index rises by 50 per cent, then the value of the index should also rise by 50 per cent. An index based on this methodology is called an 'arithmetic calculation'.

»Example (cont.)

If the initial index value in the above example was 100 then the new index values are:

- *Scenario 1*

$$100 \times \frac{10,250,000}{5,500,000} = 186.36$$

- *Scenario 2*

$$100 \times \frac{3,500,000}{5,500,000} = 63.64$$

The criteria that the index should emulate the performance of the holdings in the index also means that the index calculations cannot be for a constant life.

»Example

If the constituents of an index do not change in any way during a month—and the prices and the amounts in issue do not change—then, at the end of the month, the average life of the constituents must be one month less than at the beginning.

It was decided that, in order to emulate a portfolio, the indices should be calculated on an arithmetical basis, with fluctuating average life expectations.

Allowing for change

Any indices that are calculated must allow for the constituents to change in a seamless way. For example, there must be the ability to add new issues, to remove old issues because they are redeemed or called, and to change the amount in issue of a bond, e.g. when a further tranche is issued or it is partially called. Such changes in the constituents, while the prices are unchanged, should not cause the index calculations to jump.

A chain-link calculation method adequately solves this problem. By this method, today's index value is defined to be the previous calculation times the aggregate percentage change in the value of the current constituents since the previous calculation.

»Example

Assume the calculated price index on 31st October was 110. On the 1st November it is decided that the index now consists of two bonds A and B, which have the same amount in issue outstanding (N).

The prices of bond A on the 31st October and 1st November are 90 and 91 and, for bond B, 100 and 99½ respectively.

The value of the price index on 1st November is:

$$110 \times \frac{91 \times N + 99\frac{1}{2} \times N}{90 \times N + 100 \times N} = 110.29$$

This calculation makes no assumptions about the constituents of the index on 31st October.

This chain-link method must be adapted to allow the constituent bonds to change their issue size. (This can occur when a new tranche is issued which is fungible with it). This is achieved by weighting both the current and previous prices by the amount in issue at the previous date.

»Example

Taking the previous example, assume that the amount in issue of bond A rises from Ecu 100m on 31st October to Ecu 200m on the 1st November, and that bond B has Ecu 100m issued throughout.

Cont.

(cont.)

The index calculation on 1st November is:

$$110 \times \frac{91 \times 100 + 99\frac{1}{2} \times 100}{90 \times 100 + 100 \times 100} = 110.29$$

If the prices of *A* and *B* on 2nd November are 92 and 99, respectively, then the index on 2nd November is:

$$110.29 \times \frac{92 \times 200 + 99 \times 100}{91 \times 200 + 99\frac{1}{2} \times 100} = 110.88$$

As can be seen, this type of formula allows one to change the weights attached to each bond, and to add and subtract bonds at any time. If a bond is redeemed, or drops from the index for any reason, the formula in effect reinvests the proceeds in all the other bonds in the index in proportion to their size. For a new issue, the opposite process occurs.

Indices using the chain-link process can be calculated with any desired frequency. Although the weights associated with the constituent bonds are usually adjusted on the day they take effect, there is nothing to imply that the bond selection should be revised at a similar frequency.

Reviewing the basket of bonds

The question arises of how often one should review the basket of bonds in an index. The options available vary from every day to never—the latter option being clearly unacceptable as it would not allow the indices to continue to reflect the current market position.

At the other extreme, the 'daily' option can be rejected since the position of trading in new issues tends to vary from market to market and selecting the issues in the case of some of the indices could be quite an extensive exercise, which would be hard to justify on such a daily basis.

Domestic French indices are already calculated by the Comité de Normalisation Obligataire (CNO) in a similar way. For these indices, the basket of bonds is reviewed every 6 months, although a reduction in this period is under consideration.

It was felt that a three- or six-month period between reviewing the bonds in the index was too long as it does not adequately allow for the new issue market where new bonds are frequently the most liquid and volatile. Hence, it was agreed that a more satisfactory period would be monthly. During the monthly period, bonds would not normally be added to—or deleted from—the index. Occasions may arise where bonds have to be removed, such as when the bond goes into default, or prices cease to be available.

Bonds would be selected at the end of a calendar month for inclusion in an index on the first business day of the next month.

Frequency of calculations

The formulae described can be applied to indices being calculated at different frequencies. Although the Bloomberg/EFFAS indices, the Datastream bond indices and the ISMA eurobond indices are being calculated on a daily weekday basis, the formulae apply just as well to indices being calculated on a weekly or a monthly basis.

The formulae can also be applied to calculations being made several times a day. However, in this case, care must be taken with any chain-linking to ensure that dividends etc. are not counted more than once.

For indices calculated on a daily basis, it is conventional to ignore weekends, although the formulae will still work if this is not done.

For example, if the last calculation was based on Friday 15th, then the following calculation will normally be for Monday 18th. However, if the Monday is a bank holiday, it will be for Tuesday 19th.

Choice of price and settlement date

The choice of which prices should be used in calculating daily indices and average values was considered. Possible options included opening prices, closing prices, the latest after-hours prices, prices taken at a specific time for all indices, and average prices.

It was felt that selecting a specific time for collecting the prices of all markets, even in Europe, was not practical. (What time would be appropriate for the Japanese, US and UK government bond markets?) In addition, market-makers were more used to collecting and disseminating closing, rather than opening, prices in most markets. These tend to represent more recent information, as indices are frequently calculated overnight. On the other hand, the latest 'after-hours' prices represent even later market conditions, although the price information may be patchy and refer to different times for different securities—which may vary from day to day. The other possibility, that of an average price derived from the trades and quotations during the day, is an option where the definition could be subject to a considerable amount of controversy, while not offering any advantage over the other alternatives. (For example, should such an average take all trades to be of equal weight, or weight them by size, or give a larger weight to ones later in the day?). In addition, in many markets it is impossible to calculate an average price as the relevant trade data is not available.

As a result, it was felt that, for daily indices, prices taken at close of the official market or close of trading in that country should be used if possible.

In some markets, two-way bid and offered prices are quoted for bonds. In such cases, it is recommended that any index and associated calculations are based on the middle prices. Thus the calculations are equally valid for both buyers and sellers, and it enables bonds with greatly different spreads to be included in the same index. Similarly it helps to reduce distortions if market-makers change their spreads, as sometimes happens.

When a bond is purchased or sold, the accrued interest at the settlement date is included in the consideration paid or received. Hence, it is desirable to include the accrued interest, calculated according to the market conventions, to the normal settlement date in the calculations, with any coupons received being included when the settlement date is the same as the coupon payment date. Any distortion caused by assuming different 'normal' settlement dates, when comparing indices in different markets, is likely to be reduced in the future following a world-wide move to implement the G30 recommendation of shortening the settlement period to be within three business days of the trade.

»Examples

■ Settlement date

UK gilt-edged	Trade date +1
German bonds	Trade date +2
Italian bonds	Trade date +3
Eurobonds	Currently trade date +7 calendar days, but looking at trade date +3.

In theory, this means that the index should anticipate future payments from coupons and redemptions and reinvest the proceeds the normal number of days before settlement in the remaining securities. In practice, this would be very difficult, and so it is not done—especially as any theoretical deviations should normally cancel each other out over time.

»Example

A bond in an index where 3-day settlement is the norm, is expected to pay a coupon on Thursday 15th November. The fund manager could purchase the extra securities on Monday 12th February, so that the settlement coincides with the coupon payment. Between the 12th and the 15th of February, the price of the securities could rise or fall, although on average the effect is expected to be neutral over time.

Similarly, the life, duration and redemption yields are calculated from the normal settlement date.

Treatment of non-working days

It should be noted that, if a payment falls due on a weekend or bank holiday, then it is normal for the payment not to be received until the next business day, with the result that any monies cannot be reinvested in the index until then. The chain-link nature of the index means that it will allow for this if it is only calculated on business days.

An index on a weekend or bank holiday is, by convention, assumed to be the same as that on the previous business day, although interest normally continues to accrue. Hence, it is possible to compare UK and US indices on, for example, Columbus Day, which is a holiday in the US, but not in the UK.

Methodological conclusion

To summarize the previous discussions, it was felt that, for the indices and associated calculations,

- the indices should be based on arithmetic, and not geometric, calculations;

- the constituents should be weighted by their size (i.e. outstanding nominal value) so as to emulate a portfolio;

- the indices should allow for change by using a chain-link methodology (i.e. today's values are based on the previous value times the changes since the previous calculations);

- the constituents of an index or sub-index should be reviewed on a monthly basis;

- the indices should ideally be calculated on each business day;

- mid-market closing prices should be used if possible;

- the calculations should be based on the normal settlement date for the market.

The range of the calculations

The investment objectives for a tax-free pension fund are somewhat different to those of a money market fund, and hence the type of securities in
which they invest are different. It is not sufficient just to calculate one index
for a market and assume that everyone can compare themselves against it.
Similarly, it must be possible to adjust the published values for one's own
tax rates and imposed external cashflows.

Various calculations including a clean price index which shows the capital performance and a total return index, which includes the gross reinvested coupons can be made. These calculations must be backed up by a
variety of other indicators, so that an investor can ascertain how his portfolio differs from the index against which it is being compared.

It is self evident that calculating a clean price index on its own is not
sufficient to indicate whether a fund manager has performed well or not,
even if the bond universe is identical. For example, if the market is yielding
9 per cent, say, and has an average coupon of 9 per cent but there are some
stocks with a coupon of 5 per cent, then a price index consisting only of the
5 per cent stocks will tend to outperform the universe since there is an
inherent capital growth of circa 4 per cent per annum.

Similarly, if interest rates fall, then an index with a long duration will
tend to rise more than one with a short duration, and vice versa.

As a result it is proposed to calculate the following for each basket of
securities:

- Clean price index — it is assumed that the bonds are either quoted
  without any accrued interest, or that the implicit interest has been
  stripped out of the price. This ignores any income received.

- Gross price index — the clean price index which has been grossed
  up for the average accrued interest in the prices. (For any bond, the
  gross price is the clean price plus the accrued interest).

- Total return index — this assumes that all coupons received are
  reinvested in the index.

- Interest paid this year — This is the gross amount of interest received this year, which is reset to 0 at the beginning of each year. It
  may be used in conjunction with the total return index to allow for
  the fact that the investor may be subject to income and withholding
  tax.

In addition, the following average values, which help to describe the selected basket, are evaluated. They are:

- Average coupon
- Average life
- Average duration
- Average convexity
- Average redemption yield
- Average current yield

In each case, the constituent bond values are suitably weighted to reflect their size.

Some bonds have call and/or put options, with the result that the expected life can change according to the bond's price and assumptions about the actions of the investors and borrowers. In the case of a call option, it is assumed that the issuer will always behave in his own best interest, that is, he will call it if he can refinance the debt at a lower cost. In practice, this is assumed if the market price of the issue is above the call price. Similarly, the investor will exercise a put option if it is in his own best interest. The assumptions about call and put options have an effect not only on the average redemption yield, but also on the average life, duration, and convexity.

ONLY DATASTREAM HUNTS DOWN DATA FROM OVER 300 SOURCES WORLDWIDE

International banks and stock exchanges, financial publications and government statistical offices: some of the big game Datastream tracks down to bring you the most comprehensive and up-to-date financial market data possible.

Global Focus. Because we hunt all over the world, we're able to bring you equity, company and bond prices and market data from 35 countries. As well as economic data from 130, forex, interest rates and indices from 27 and company accounts from 22 countries.

Accurate. Data from virtually every source is checked and validated by our 120 strong team, then endorsed by our unique Data Guarantee.

Powerful. With user-friendly access through a full Windows™ environment. It's ideal for downloading, multi-tasking, graphics manipulation and integrated desk-top publishing.

For more information contact Datastream Sales on (071) 250 3000.

™ Windows is a registered trademark of Microsoft Corporation.

A **PRIMARK** Company

Datastream International

LONDON · NEW YORK · TOKYO · HONG KONG
PARIS · FRANKFURT · ROTTERDAM · ZURICH · SYDNEY

Chapter 4

Types of bond index

Initially, the main interest in creating universally-accepted indices across markets was so that it was possible to compare the performance of different government bond markets. This was partly because, not only were the government bond markets the most homogeneous sector, but they were also the most actively traded. However, the following proposals may be just as readily applied to other areas, such as government-guaranteed, public sector, corporate sector, banks, supranationals, eurobonds etc., or even to the total country bond market.

It was recognized that there were various users of bond indices who all had different requirements. For example, domestic investors—being long-term investors, whose portfolio would tend to encompass both liquid and illiquid bonds—require an index that covers all the sector and would therefore appreciate an 'All-bond' index. However, since price collection in some sections of a country's market may be difficult, a proxy for an All-bond index, which depends on a sample of bonds yet tracks the All-bond index well, is needed. This is referred to as the 'Tracker' index.

International investors, on the other hand, are often more interested in the most liquid bonds in a sector. The index formed of such bonds is referred to as the 'Bellwether' index. It is felt that the constituents of a Bellwether index should always be contained in the Tracker index.

Thus, as shown in Figure 1 overleaf, for any market there can be three bond indices: an All-bond index, a Tracker index and a Bellwether index. However, as soon as you move outside the government bond area, it may not be practical to calculate all three indices.

All-bond index

Since investors have the opportunity to invest in all bonds, their decisions to exclude or overweight particular bonds, or types of bond, should be rewarded. Therefore, if an investor decides to hold high-coupon bonds, or bonds of a particular type, such as callable, index-linked, 'flower' bonds, etc.—assuming he is allowed to hold them—any under, or over, performance should be measurable and identified and the manager rewarded accordingly.

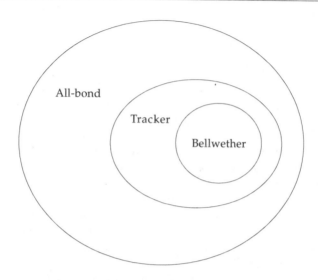

Figure 1   Bond universe selection

It is recommended that the All-bond indices should include all compara-ble eligible bonds in the market. Reasons for including, and excluding, spe-cific bonds are discussed in Chapter 7.

Since price collection and liquidity are frequently a problem, All-bond indices will often only be calculated for the government sector, although they may be calculated for other sectors in some markets.

As indicated above, an All-bond government bond index is probably most suitable for funds based in that country, since such funds have a wider range of securities and often hold illiquid issues.

Tracker bond index

Several market related criteria were considered as the basis for selecting bonds for the Tracker and the Bellwether indices from the All-bond uni-verse. These were:

i) Market value

The largest bonds, as measured by market value, tend on the whole to be the most liquid and represent the performance of the market. Market value is also a measure that is relatively stable, compared with some other criteria, and readily calculable, provided the amount in issue is known and there is a price.

It is a better measure than the amount in issue, since it allows one to compare issues with different coupons and lives.

It is recommended that market value is one of the main criteria used in selecting both the Tracker and Bellwether constituents.

ii) Turnover

Should bonds with a turnover of less than a specified amount be excluded or not? It was felt that this was not a satisfactory selection criterion, as the figures can vary enormously over time for a specific bond (e.g. in the euro-bond market, most of the trading in a bond occurs in the first few months of its life), and the official figures frequently only represent a small fraction of the total market turnover, as in Austria.

iii) Price quality

It is desirable to include in an index only those securities for which 'trade-able' prices are available. In some, but not all, markets it is possible to quantify the quality of the prices.

» Example

In the eurobond market, the quality of the price increases if you specify that the average spread between the bid and offered price is less than a certain amount, and this price range is constructed from the prices given by at least a minimum number of market-makers.

Such a price quality restriction would seem to be a valid selection criterion.

iv) Rating

There are various credit rating agencies (e.g. Standard and Poor's and Moody's) which rate the ability of issuers to repay both the capital and interest on the loan. Unfortunately, no credit rating agency covers the markets comprehensively. This can be illustrated by the fact that Republic of France BTAN and German government issues do not have a rating. In addition, the issues of some organizations have different ratings due to different terms, structures, or rankings of bondholders in case of default. If a bond issued by an organization is rated, it is not possible to assume that all bonds issued by the same organization are similarly rated.

»Example

■ Crédit Foncier de France US dollar bonds were differently rated by both Standard & Poor's and Moody's in October 1993

	Moody's	Standard & Poor's
8% 1991-2002	AA1	AA+
9½% 1989-1999	Aaa	AAA

This rating difference was, in fact, caused by the fact that the higher coupon bond has a French government guarantee whereas more recent issues such as the 8% do not.

There is an argument for only including bonds with a rating of, say, at least 'A', on the grounds that the excluded bonds may not be of satisfactory investment grade. Such an approach, as has been pointed out, would exclude BTAN and similar issues from the calculations, but may be valid in some markets.

v) Yield variations

Another possible criterion for removing a security from an index group is that, when the selection was made, it did not have a redemption yield that was comparable to that of the other bonds in the selection.

The French bond indices produced by the Comité de Normalisation Obligataire do reject those bonds with a redemption yield which is more than two standard deviations away from the average one. This works very well in what is essentially a homogeneous market.

However, if such an approach is used, the following should be considered:

• The market may not be homogeneous, as is the case in some of the eurobond ones, e.g. it could consist on the one hand of World Bank issues and, on the other, of speculative corporate or Third World borrowers.

»Example

Such a situation occurred in the compilation of the eurobond Swiss franc indices where the yield on one large issue was about three times that of the rest of the market. The bond was not in default, but the market was obviously worried about the issuer's ability to meet his obligations. The inclusion of this bond had a

Cont.

(cont.)

significant effect on the Tracker index, where the average yield was increased by nearly 1 per cent. Unfortunately, this problem was compounded since it was, according to the rules, included one month, not the next, then included again the following month. The problem was removed by introducing a maximum yield of not more than 5% above or twice the average for the group.

- The yield curve may not be reasonably flat, with the result that a security may be rejected solely because it has a different maturity expectation to the other issues in the index.

    One way round this would be to fit a yield curve to the potential constituents and measure the deviation from the curve, rather than from an average. The yield curve itself does not need to be particularly sophisticated since it is only being used to reject deviant securities—all of which have a life of at least one year. (A simple cubic curve would probably suffice).

- Care must be taken to use the correct yield for bonds which have calls, puts etc.

    Based on the assumption that both the issuer and the investor will act in their own best interest, in the case of a callable bond, a yield to call, as opposed to maturity, will be calculated if it pays the issuer to call the bond. From an investor's point of view, this is called a 'yield to worst'.

For government Tracker bond indices, it was felt that such market yield considerations were not necessary, although they may be desirable in other markets.

Whenever such restrictions are placed on the bond selections they should be explicitly stated.

Recommendation ➤   It is recommended that the bonds to be used in calculating the Tracker index are selected from those in the equivalent All-bond index as follows:

- First of all, some bonds with special features, or no liquidity, are removed from the potential sample.

- Bonds are then selected in order of decreasing market value (i.e. normally clean price x amount outstanding/100), until either:

- 20 or more bonds have been selected and at least 25 per cent of the group by market value has been covered,

  or:

- more than 50 per cent of the group by market value has been covered.

In addition, any bonds representing more than 5 per cent of the market, and any being an identical size to the smallest selected bond are included.

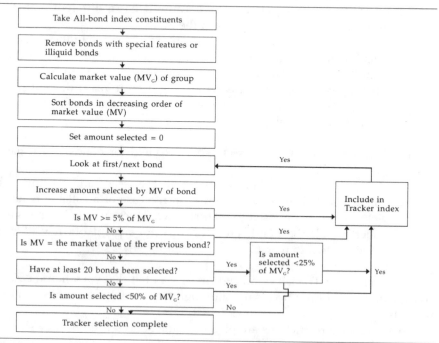

Figure 2   Flow diagram for selecting Tracker index constituents

The Tracker index is considered the most appropriate for all professional investors, whether domestic or international. It covers the range of securities available and not just the latest benchmark issues. By encompassing large issues, it tracks the market accurately and allows securities with unique features to be excluded.

Note: Market value is a better selection criterion than amount outstanding, as it makes long-dated, high- and zero-coupon bonds directly comparable.

A method very similar to this is already used for selecting bonds for the French Comité de Normalisation Obligataire (CNO) indices.

Bellwether bond index

For international investors, an index that covers only very liquid issues is the most appropriate one, since they are rarely long-term investors. In some markets (such as those for Japanese government bonds and US Treasuries) a large proportion of the trading is done in the latest benchmark issue(s). Constructing an index which consists solely of the benchmark issues was rejected in favour of the Bellwether index described below. The reasons for this were:

- The selection of the benchmark might not be completely objective, especially when one benchmark is being replaced by another, making the index difficult to reproduce.

- The new benchmark could have different characteristics to the old one, producing problems of continuity, etc.

- In some market sectors, there could be an interregnum between benchmark issues.

The major problem with any Bellwether index is still that its constituent bonds are constantly changing, giving rise to concerns about any continuous series of values.

It was felt that the selection of the individual bonds in the Bellwether index ought to be according to some objective criteria.

Turnover was rejected as an objective criterion, since this number can be very difficult to obtain in many markets. For example, in Austria the official stock exchange figures are meaningless, since only 3-5 per cent of the turnover occurs on the exchange. In addition, difficulties arise due to the problem of differentiating between retail and market-maker turnover.

In the eurobond market, it has been found that a very good indication of liquidity is the number of market-makers who report daily prices to the ISMA as published in ISMA's *Weekly Eurobond Guide*. This is, in fact, a better indication of liquidity than the size of the issue or the price quotation spread.

After consideration, it was decided to select the constituents of the Bellwether index from those of the Tracker index as shown in Figure 3, overleaf.

Recommendation ➤   Up to 5 securities will be chosen for the Bellwether Index according to the following prioritized selection criteria:

- Greatest number of market-makers, if appropriate for the market;

- The price spread must be less than the average for the Tracker index, unless they are all the same;

- Market value.

In the event of more than one issue having the same market value the latest issue will be selected.

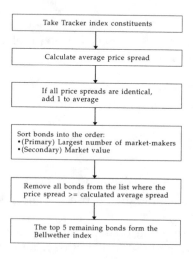

Figure 3   Flow diagram for selecting Bellwether index constituents

Chapter 5

Maturity sub-groups

It is not particularly useful for a portfolio manager to compare his performance with an index which has a much shorter or longer time horizon than his portfolio; pension funds, for example, often have a long-term horizon. As a result, it was considered desirable to calculate indices and average values for bonds with similar maturity expectations, in addition to the total market calculations.

There are several different measures of maturity expectation that could be used in deciding how to divide the bond universe. The criteria considered included: life to final maturity, average life, equivalent life, life to call or put, duration, modified duration and 'operative' life, which is derived from the other criteria.

Life to final maturity

The life of a bond from now until final maturity is a simple easy to understand concept, but it does have its limitations if the bond is not a bullet.

Even for a bullet, it is not a perfect measure, since it makes no allowance for coupon payments.

»Example

Consider two bonds A and B which are both redeemed in 10 years time at par. Bond A has a 10 per cent annual coupon, whereas bond B is a zero-coupon one.

During the next 10 years, bond A will pay out coupons to the value of 100 per cent of the nominal capital, with the result that the average period to payout of all future cashflows is:

$$= \frac{10}{200} \times (1 + 2 + 3 + .. + 10) + \frac{100}{200} \times 10$$

$= 7.75$ years

On the other hand, bond B has an average life of 10 years, since no payments are made prior to redemption.

Average life

In the case of serial bonds, which are redeemed over a number of years, life to final maturity is not a particularly useful measure of the life of the bond, since a significant proportion of the investment will have been redeemed by then.

The average life of a bond is defined to be the period from the value-date to the average of the future sinking fund dates, weighted by the non-discounted repayments.

»Example

If a bond has a sinking fund of:

20 per cent to be redeemed on 1/6/1998 at par
10 per cent to be redeemed on 1/6/1999 at par
70 per cent to be redeemed on 1/6/2000 at par

Then the average life on 1/6/1993 can be calculated as follows:

$$\text{Average life} = \frac{20 \times 5 + 10 \times 6 + 70 \times 7}{20 + 10 + 70} = 6.5 \text{ years}$$

i.e. the average redemption date is 1/12/1999.

For a bullet bond, the average life is the same as the life to maturity.

Equivalent life

The equivalent life of a serial bond is very similar to that of average life, except that, now, the capital repayments are discounted at the redemption yield rate. Earlier payouts are worth more to the investor than identical later ones, since they can be reinvested.

»Example

Using the same example as for average life, assume the bond is priced at 100 and has an annual coupon of 8 per cent on 1/6/1993. Hence, it has a redemption yield of 8 per cent.

The equivalent life e of the bond is now given by solving:

$$(20 + 10 + 70) \times v^e = 20 \times v^5 + 10 \times v^6 + 70 \times v^7$$

where v (the discount factor) $= \frac{1}{(1 + 0.08)}$ as the yield is 8 per cent

Cont.

(cont.)

This formula gives:

$$v^e = .60758$$
$$e = 6.4744 \text{ years}$$

i.e. the equivalent life is slightly shorter than the average life.

Equivalent life was rejected as a maturity measure since, although it reflects the real world better than average life, two bonds with identical redemption schedules will have different equivalent lives if they do not yield the same[1]. This could put them in different maturity sub-groups.

Life to call or put

The life to call is the period from the value-date to the first call opportunity, taking into account the notice period the issuer must give the holders. Similarly, the life to put is the period to the first put option date.

In some cases, where the call or put option prices vary over time, the life to call or put may be taken to a subsequent option date. This occurs when it is in the best interest of the holder of the option. In practice, the most appropriate date for such a bond can be derived by calculating the return to each date and comparing with yields of similar bullet bonds. This is necessary to take account of the yield curve structure at any one time.

Operative life

The operative life is the average life of a bond adjusted for options on the assumption that both the issuer and investor act in their own best interest. Hence for a callable bond, a 'yield to worst' calculation is performed, assuming that the issuer will exercise his most advantageous option. The life calculation is based on the redemption date which gives the 'worst' yield for the holder, i.e. if the yield to call is less than the yield to redemption, then it is assumed that the bond will be called, and so has a life which reflects the call and not the redemption. Similarly, for a puttable bond, or a bond which is extendible at the holder's option, a 'yield to best' is calcu-

---

[1] *In order to avoid the problem of identical redemption schedules being treated differently, it would theoretically be possible to discount them all at some average market rate over a large number of years, instead of at the redemption rate yield, when calculating an equivalent life. This approach is rejected since, even if market rates are available, they may not be representative of the current situation.*

lated, assuming that the bondholder will exercise his most advantageous option. The life calculation is now based on the date which gives the best yield for the holder.

In the above cases, the operative life of bond is obviously a better measure of life than life to maturity, although, in the case of callable and puttable bonds, the expected life can change when the price, and hence the yield, changes.

It should be noted that when a bond moves from the assumption that it will be redeemed at maturity to being called or put, there is no large jump in its redemption yield. However, as will be seen later, there is a jump in the average redemption yield of the index group, since the operative life of the bond has jumped.

Duration

The concept of duration is a better measure of the life of an investment than life to maturity, or average, or equivalent life, as it takes into account both the coupon and the redemption payments. Duration is defined to be the average life of the present values of all future cashflows from the bond. In calculating the present value of the future cashflows, a discount rate equal to the redemption yield of the bond is used.

»Formula — Duration (Macaulay)

The duration D of a bond is given by:

$$D = \frac{\displaystyle\sum_{i=1}^{n} CF_i \times L_i \times v^{L_i}}{\displaystyle\sum_{i=1}^{n} CF_i \times v^{L_i}}$$

where,

n	number of future coupon and capital cashflows
CF_i	ith future cashflow
L_i	time in years to the ith cashflow
v	annualized discounting factor

i.e. if the annualized yield is y then $v = \dfrac{1}{(1+y)}$

($y = 0.08$ for a yield of 8 per cent)

Cont.

(cont.)

However, since the gross price P (i.e. clean price plus accrued interest) of a bond is the present value of all future cashflows, we can write:

$$P = \sum_{i=1}^{n} CF_i \times v^{L_i}$$

This is the general redemption yield formula. As a result, the duration formula may be simplified to:

$$D = \frac{1}{P} \times \sum_{i=1}^{n} CF_i \times L_i \times v^{L_i}$$

The resulting calculation is sometimes referred to as the Macaulay duration.

This unfortunately means that the duration of a bond is dependent on its price, and that two bonds with identical cashflows could be in different sub-groups.

»Example (i)

The average duration of the discounted cashflows of a 10-year bond yielding 10 per cent with a 10 per cent coupon is 6.76 years, whereas that of a 10-year zero-coupon bond is still 10 years. Thus, the latter has a duration which is 1.48 times as long as the former. Hence they may be classified into different maturity sub-groups.

»Example (ii)

Consider 2 bonds A and B on 1st July 1993 with 8 per cent annual coupons. They are both redeemed on 1st July 1999 at par, but have different credit ratings.

Bond A has a price of 105, which produces a duration of 5.02, whereas bond B has a price of 95, and a duration of 4.96.

As a result, they may be put into different maturity sub-groups, although they have identical projected future cashflows. Can this be right?

Another problem associated with using duration as a measure of life is the fact that it does not decrease smoothly from now until final redemption. This could mean that a bond could move from one maturity band to another and back again without there being a change of price or yield. It should be noted that, in the case of serial bonds, this occurs with the average life and equivalent life calculations as well on a partial redemption date.

»Example

Figure 4 shows how the duration of a bond which pays an annual coupon of 10 per cent changes over its 8-year life assuming the price remains at par.

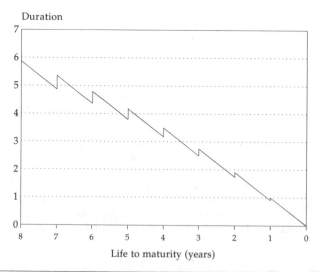

Figure 4   **The changes in duration of a 10% bond, assuming price remains at par**

In particular, it will be seen that the duration moves from above 5, to below 5, then back above 5 and below 5 again over time.

Modified duration

The modified duration of a bond ranks securities according to their price sensitivity to yield changes. The modified duration of a bond is sometimes referred to as its volatility. However, this term should not be confused with its use with options. Mathematically, the modified duration is just the duration of the bond multiplied by the redemption yield discounting factor.

»Formula — Modified duration

The modified duration MD of a bond is given by:

$$MD = -\frac{dP}{dy} \times \frac{1}{P}$$

where,

P gross price (i.e. clean price plus accrued interest)
dP small change in price
dy corresponding small change in yield

As already stated, the gross price of a bond is the present value of all the future cashflows associated with the bond, i.e.

$$P = \sum_{i=1}^{n} CF_i \times v^{Li}$$

where,

n number of future coupon and capital cashflows
CF_i ith future cashflow
L_i time in years to the ith cashflow
v annualized discounting factor

      i.e. if the annualized yield is y then $v = \dfrac{1}{(1+y)}$

      ($y = 0.08$ for a yield of 8 per cent)

$$\frac{dP}{dy} = \frac{dP}{dv} \times \frac{dv}{dy}$$

$$= \frac{dv}{dy} \times \sum_{i=1}^{n} CF_i \times L_i \times v^{Li-1}$$

$$= -v^2 \times \sum_{i=1}^{n} CF_i \times L_i \times v^{Li-1}$$

Hence,

$$MD = v \times \frac{1}{P} \times \sum_{i=1}^{n} CF_i \times L_i \times v^{Li}$$

$$= v \times D$$

where,

D duration (see previous section)

Modified duration[1] is not the type of restriction that is usually put on portfolio managers, and so will not be considered further as a measure of life, since it still has the inherent problems associated with duration.

The different measures of life can be illustrated by the following example:

»Example

Consider, on 1st July 1993, the following bond which pays an annual coupon of 8 per cent on 1st July each year and is priced at 100. On the 1st July 1995, it is callable at 100 on 30 days' notice at the company's option. The bond will normally be redeemed in two equal tranches at 100 on 1st July 1996 and 1997.

For this bond, we have:

Redemption yield:	8.00 per cent
Life to maturity:	4 years (to 1/7/1997)
Average life:	3.5 years (to 1/1/1997)
Equivalent life:	3.48 years. This is slightly under 3.5 years, since the present value of the redemption in 1997 is less than that in 1996)
Life to call:	2 years (to 1/1/1995)
Operative life:	3.5 years, i.e. to average life since the yield to call is not less than yield to maturity. However, if the price were over 100 it may pay the issuer (ignoring expenses) to call the bond. Hence, the operative life would be 2 years
Duration (Macaulay):	3.18 years
Modified duration:	2.94

Other considerations

Bonds have been issued with a variety of other features. For example, some bonds have purchase funds. Its operation is an event usually contingent on the bonds trading below par. Its effect is therefore to support the price, but

---

[1] *Modified duration is used by the French 'Commission des Opérations de Bourse' to inform buyers of mutual funds of the rate exposure of their investments.*

the timing of its operation is unpredictable. The existence of such a fund does not normally affect the long-term return to an investor, or affect its expected life or duration, and so may be ignored in the calculations.

Indices can also be constructed to give either a constant life or duration, but such calculations do not reflect the performance of an average holder. Hence, it is to measure the performance of the market sector as if it were a portfolio which is recommended for both the total market indices and sub-indices based on some maturity measure.

Choice of maturity measure

From the discussion above, it can be seen that the choice for the maturity subdivision basis is between operative life and duration. The relevant factors are:

- The duration gives a better measure of the period of the outstanding cashflows of the security than operative life;

- The duration calculations are dependent on the yield of the bond, and so change as the price moves. This also occurs with operative life in the case of callable/puttable bonds. It means that a bond can (theoretically) move from one maturity group to another, and back again, as prices change;

- The duration of a bond increases on a coupon payout date (or ex-dividend date);

- Market yield shifts can cause all the bonds within one duration band to move to another—for example, irredeemable bonds...
  yielding 15%, have a duration of 6.67 years
  yielding 10%, have a duration of 10 years
  and, yielding 5%, have a duration of 20 years;

- The market and trustees tend to group bonds with like final maturities together.

Recommendation ➤   It is this final point of market practice, together with the fact that it is obvious into which sub-group a bond will go, that has meant it is recommended that the sub-groups be based on 'operative life' as opposed to duration. However, it does not mean that indices cannot be calculated based on duration sub-divisions.

Suggested maturity sub-divisions

After some discussion it was decided that for the Government domestic bond indices, in addition to the total index calculations, sub-indices should be calculated for bonds with operative lives in the following bands.

- 1 — 3 years
- 3 — 5 years
- 5 — 7 years
- 7 — 10 years
- Over 10 years
- Irredeemable securities

Please note that the calculations for bonds with a life to maturity of less than one year are different. (*See* Chapter 12, Money/cash market indices).

However, it is recognized that all these sub-divisions are not applicable to indices in every market; for example, before mid-1993 there were no Portuguese escudo eurobonds with a life to maturity of over five years. Similarly, there are very few securities in some other subdivisions. As a result, in some markets (such as that for eurobonds), larger maturity groupings may be deemed desirable. In fact, for eurobonds, ISMA calculates indices for all maturities greater than 1 year, 1-5 years, and over 5 years.

It should be noted that it is possible to combine indices together to form larger groupings.

Chapter 6

Treatment of events

Although, as has been discussed, the constituents of an index group normally remain unchanged during each selection period (that is, during the month), various events can occur for which allowance must be made. Some of these events are discussed below.

Bonds being quoted ex-coupon or ex-dividend

In some markets, bonds start to be quoted without the next coupon payment some time before the payment date. This situation is frequently referred to as the price being quoted ex-coupon or ex-dividend (XD). Markets where bonds go XD include the Danish, Irish, Swedish and UK domestic markets.

»Examples

The calculation of when bonds go XD varies, not only from market to market, but sometimes also from bond to bond.

- ■ UK gilt-edged market

Most gilts go ex-dividend when the settlement date is 37 days before the coupon date, or the next business day. However, stocks which pay coupons on the 5th, 6th, 7th or 8th of January, April, July or October (such as Consols 2½%) go ex-dividend on the first business day of the preceding month.

- ■ Danish domestic bond market

Danish bonds trade ex-dividend when the value date falls within the period of 30 calendar days before the interest due date.

During this period, the bonds are purchased and sold with negative accrued interest, and hence the gross price of a bond during this period is less than the clean price. The original holder is entitled to the next coupon even if he sells the security.

»Example

Consider a bond with an annual 6% coupon payable on 1st June. If it goes XD on the 1st May, and the clean price of the bond is 90 throughout the period, the gross price (i.e. the price including accrued interest) will be shown as in Figure 5 below.

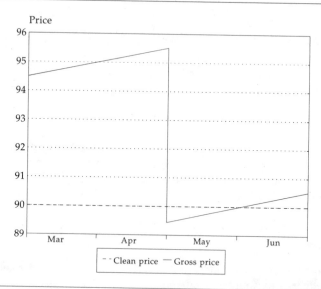

Figure 5   An example of the gross price movement of a bond going XD

N.B. In some markets, the clean price tends to rise slightly on the XD date due to tax reasons.

The normal formulae for calculating the sector gross price index, redemption yield, duration and convexity figures work satisfactorily when a bond is quoted XD. However, the total return index needs to specifically allow for such occasions, since the value of the holding does not decrease when the security starts to be quoted XD and the coupon is not available for reinvestment until the payment date.

Processing cashflows

The constituents of an index or portfolio normally create cashflows in the form of coupon payments and redemptions. Conversely, they may absorb cashflows when a call is paid on a partly-paid security, or a new issue is added. Receipts from coupon payments are ignored when calculating the clean price index, although redemptions, etc. still need to be accounted for.

The question arises as to how one should invest these cashflows. For the purpose of the discussion, it is assumed that cashflows are only created. Various options are possible.

i)   Remove the proceeds from the calculation.

ii) Put the proceeds into an included 'cash' stock which does not earn any interest.

iii) Put the proceeds into an included 'cash' stock which earns interest at an appropriate rate.

iv) In the case of a coupon payment, for the total return index, reinvest the proceeds ignoring any transaction costs in the security that produced the cashflow. A different procedure is obviously required for the final redemption of a security.

v)   Reinvest the proceeds in the index constituents according to their weights. All theoretical transaction costs are ignored.

The *first* option is satisfactory if you only want to calculate an index which measures your capital performance, while ignoring any income. It is thus not the basis for a total return index, although it could be used for a clean price index if allowances are made for changes in constituents.

The *second* option is unsatisfactory since, over time, the cash element could become large, although it could be reinvested at the beginning of the next month when the constituent bonds are reviewed. This would have the effect of dampening the index movements, and does not reflect any return on this money. Such an index would perform better than the market in a bear market, and worse in a bull market.

The *third* option, although an improvement on the second, means that an external rate of interest has to be chosen—and specified. Is this an overnight, 7-day, or even 3-month rate? This is contrary to the basic principle that external factors should not affect the performance of an index group.

Another approach would be to assume that the cash accrues interest at the average coupon rate of the index. This again has its limitations since such returns may not be realizable.

»Example

■ If you look at the UK gilt-edged securities 5-7 year index in October 1993, you will see that the coupons of the bonds vary from 9.5 per cent to 15.5 per cent, with prices of between 112 and 137, when all the bonds have redemption yields of less than 7. (All bonds being redeemable at par). At the same time, short-term money market interest rates were somewhat less than this.

The *fourth* option—whereby coupons are reinvested in the security which produced the cashflow—has limitations, since the performance of the index would now be dependent on the base date of the index.

»Example

Consider an index consisting of 1000 units of securities A and B at time t_0. At time t_2, A pays a coupon of 10 per cent which is reinvested in itself. The total return index is calculated between time t_0 and time t_3. During this time security B does not pay a coupon. If the prices including any accrued interest of A and B at times t_0, t_1, t_2 and t_3 are:

Time	t_0	t_1	t_2	t_3
A	100	90	90	100
B	100	100	100	100

and the index I_0 at time t_0 is 100, then we have for the index I_1 at time t_1:

$$I_1 = I_0 \times \frac{(1000 \times 90 + 1000 \times 100)}{(1000 \times 100 + 1000 \times 100)}$$

$$= 100 \times \frac{190}{200}$$

$$= 95$$

Similarly, the index I_2 at time t_2 is given by:

$$I_2 = I_1 \times \frac{(1000 \times (90 + 10) + 1000 \times 100)}{(1000 \times 90 + 1000 \times 100)}$$

$$= 95 \times \frac{200}{190}$$

$$= 100$$

In the equation above, the 10 per cent coupon for A was added to A's price. This

Cont.

(cont.)

coupon is now reinvested in A with the result that A's capital now increases to 1100.

The calculation of the index I_3 at time t_3 is now given by:

$$I_3 = I_2 \times \frac{(1100 \times 100 + 1000 \times 100)}{(1100 \times 90 + 1000 \times 100)}$$

$$= 100 \times \frac{210}{199}$$

$$= 105.53$$

Using the same example, if an index I^* were now to be calculated with a base date of time t_2 (after security A had paid the coupon) then, as the weights of the two securities would be 1000, the calculations are now:

$$I^*_2 = 100$$

$$I^*_3 = I^*_2 \times \frac{(1000 \times 100 + 1000 \times 100)}{(1000 \times 90 + 1000 \times 100)}$$

$$= 100 \times \frac{200}{190}$$

$$= 105.26$$

This gives a different percentage movement between times t_2 and t_3 than in the previous calculation, and so is unsatisfactory.

In the above example, of the index with a base date at time t_0, an investor entering the market at time t_3 has no reason for buying more bonds of A than B, because the outstanding volume remains at 1000 in both cases and the past is of no interest to him.

Another problem associated with this approach is that, over time, securities with high coupons will get disproportionately large weightings compared with zero- or low-coupon bonds.

The *fifth* option—of reinvesting the proceeds in the index in the proportion to the size of the holdings—has none of the problems associated with the other alternatives. However, it does have the disadvantage that it is frequently not possible to implement in practice, even if all transactions costs are ignored, since one cannot purchase part of a bond. (for example, in the eurobond market, a minimum bond size of $5,000, $10,000 or even $100,000 is common). This objection does not invalidate the mathematics and, as a result, it is this option which is used. Obviously it can be used for negative cashflows as well.

External cashflows

In the previous section, we discussed how cashflows generated or absorbed by the index constituents are taken into account. In practice, all portfolio managers have external cashflow restrictions. Such restrictions are particular to each fund, and so should not be reflected in general indices. However, fund managers ought to be able to construct indices which reflect their external restrictions from the general indices.

Timing of cashflow investments

We have discussed how to treat generated or absorbed cashflows by the index constituents. The next question is when to make the investments, since in most markets it is not possible—or normal—to purchase securities for settlement on the same day. Various options exist, even for the receipt and reinvestment of coupons. The following were considered:

i)   On the coupon payment date, purchase the required securities for the normal settlement date of the market. This date varies from market to market. (For example, the UK gilt-edged market is usually the following day, while the German Bundesrepublik market is usually 2 business days and the eurobond market is currently 7 calendar days, although it is proposed to reduce this period).

   The coupon monies could:

   a) be assumed not to accrue any interest until settlement;
   b) accrue interest at the average coupon rate until settlement;
   c) be put on deposit until settlement.

ii)   The new securities could be purchased the relevant number of days before the coupon payment date, so that the coupon and settlement dates would coincide. Then, the purchase price could immediately have an in-built profit or loss, depending on the price movements during this period.

iii) The new securities could be purchased on the coupon payment date for immediate inclusion in the index.

In practice, it is expected that most investment managers will adopt policy (i) above, unless they expect the market to advance in the next few days, when they may adopt policy (ii). The problem about implementing (i) is that the calculation is dependent on agreeing an external deposit interest rate, which would make the reproduction of the indices difficult, and be against the general index calculation principles.

As a result, it was decided to adopt option (iii) which, although not practical from an investment point of view, is easy to reproduce and does not involve any subjective decisions. Option (iii) calculations, unlike those of options (i) and (ii), remove the problem associated with the market moving between the purchase and settlement dates. Over time, such movements are unlikely to be systematically cumulative in any one direction.

It should be noted that the proposed formulae reinvest the coupons on the coupon dates even when there is a period where the security is quoted ex-coupon.

Similar principles are used when considering cashflows from other causes (such as a call on a partially-paid security or a partial redemption of a serial bond). An investment or disinvestment is assumed to have immediate effect.

This approach helps in two other areas:

- It removes the problem of the cashflow date being in one selection period but the settlement date being in a different one, when the securities may have changed;

- It makes cross-market comparisons easier.

New issues

The question of how soon to add new issues to an index, when they meet all the selection criteria was discussed in detail. The possible options, which are dependent on the market, vary from immediately the issue is announced to several months after the issue date. Issues which are further tranches of existing issues are discussed later.

In some markets (eurobonds and US Treasury notes & bonds, for example), a 'grey' market is created in the bond as soon as the issue is announced. Trading in the grey market is for settlement on a 'when and if' basis. At any time up to the issue or closing date, the issue may be pulled, i.e. all the agreed grey market trades are now null and void. As a result, it is considered that such bonds should not be included before the issue or closing date, since pulled issues could distort the indices.

In other markets, new issues are offered for purchase over a long period which can be over a year (as is the case in the Danish mortgage loan market).

During this period, the amount in issue continually increases. When the amount currently in issue is known, and meets the selection criteria, it can be included in the index even if the issue is still 'open', as this fact does not alter the long-term return to an investor.

On the other hand, there are some markets where new bonds are not freely tradeable or do not become officially-quoted in the first few months of their life (for example, in Germany although new *Bundesobligationen* bonds are not officially quoted for some months, they are readily tradeable). One possible argument is to exclude bonds until this occurs. However, if this procedure were adopted, any gains or losses incurred by investors purchasing new issues would be ignored.

Similarly, since the indices are based on the principle that the bonds in an index are fixed for a calendar month, it was felt new issues should only be included at the beginning of a period.

As a result of the discussions, it was felt that a reasonable compromise which reflected the performance of new issues was to consider them for inclusion in the appropriate index at the next selection date, after the issue date, provided the amount in issue is known, and a reliable price is available, even if this is not an official quotation. Hence the initial inclusion price for a new issue is not normally the issue price.

Further tranche of an existing issue

When a further tranche of a security is created, the new tranche may be fungible immediately on payment, or possibly not for a few months. In some cases the new tranche has a different first coupon amount with the result that it cannot become fungible before the coupon date.

»Examples

■ France OAT 8% 1993-2003

An additional tranche of Ecu 500m was issued on 15 July 1993. This was immediately fungible.

■ Société Générale 9¼% 1991-99

An additional tranche of FFr 83.2m was issued on 30 April 1993 as the result of a coupon reinvestment option. The new tranche was immediately fungible.

■ European Investment Bank 7¼% Notes 1992-98

An additional tranche of C$ 200m was issued on 24 March 1993. It was fungible with the existing bond from 21 May 1993.

Before the fungible date, the new tranche is effectively a new bond and should be treated as such. After the fungible date, the amount in issue of the original bond should be increased appropriately. It is recommended that this occurs immediately, and not at the month-end. In this way, the treatment of increases and decreases in capital (*see* 'Serial bond partial redemption', later in this chapter) can be treated consistently.

Two existing tranches become fungible

Sometimes, when a new tranche of a bond is issued, it is not immediately fungible with the existing issue. A frequent reason for this is that it is entitled to a different first coupon. After this payment the two issues become fungible. When two issues become fungible the amount in issue of the ongoing issue is immediately increased to the combined capital and the size of the other issue (if it is in the index) is reduced to zero.

A slight complication can occur if the 'deceased' issue was in the index, but the ongoing issue was not. In this case, the contents of the sub-group should be switched to the ongoing issue on the fungible date.

Security not priced

If, for any reason, a security in an index is not priced today, then the following approaches are possible:

- Keep the security in the index at the last known price for a specified period, or until the prices are again available;

- Drop the security from the index and do not reinstate if prices become available again;

- Drop the security from the index and reinstate when prices are available;

- A combination of the above.

If a non-priced security is retained in the index, until either the next selection date, or when it is priced again, any index movements will be reduced by its inclusion. If the security is again priced, any deadening of the index movements will be corrected.

The option of dropping (zero weighting) the security and then reinstating when prices are available is not widely used and can lead to distortions in the calculations (see example). As a result, it is not recommended.

»Example

Consider an index consisting of two bonds, *A* and *B*, which have equal weights. The prices of the bonds on three consecutive days are:

	Day 1	Day 2	Day 3
A	100	105	105
B	100	not available	105

Using the proposed method of taking the price for B on day 2 as 100, the index calculation will be:

Index Day 1 =   100 (assumed)

Index Day 2 =   Index Day 1 x change on day

$$= 100 \times \frac{105 + 100}{100 + 100} = 102.5$$

Index Day 3 =   Index Day 2 x change on day

$$= 102.5 \times \frac{105 + 105}{105 + 100} = 105$$

It can be seen that this method gives the same Day 3 index value for any prices of bonds *A* and *B* on Day 2.

On the other hand, zero weighting *B* on Day 2, we have index calculations of:

Index Day 1 =   100 (assumed)

Index Day 2 =   Index Day 1 x change on day

$$= 100 \times \frac{105}{100} = 105$$

Index Day 3 =   Index Day 2 x change on day

$$= 105 \times \frac{105 + 105}{105 + 100} = 107.56$$

A similar problem occurs if it is decided to drop bond *B* from the index for day 2 and day 3, but reinstate it on day 4 when it has a price for yesterday as well. In this case, no allowance is made for the price rise between Days 1 and 3.

Recommendation ➤   If a security is not priced on a specific day, then the price should be assumed to be the same as on the previous business day. If the security is not priced for 3 consecutive business days, in the case of a government security index, or 5 consecutive days otherwise, the security should be dropped from the index, and should not be reinstated before the next sub-group selection at the end of the month. In some smaller markets, it may be desirable to relax the period for removing securities, especially during periods of little activity or market movement.

Security is temporarily suspended

When the quotation for a security is suspended, albeit on a temporary basis, there is often no precise statement of when trading will commence again. The security involved ceases to be priced immediately, with the result that it is removed from the index, after three days in the case of a government security, or five days otherwise. If the suspension is only temporary pending an announcement, the quotation will probably be returned within the 3- or 5-day period, with the result that the security is never removed from the index. If it is restored within the index selection period (i.e. the calendar month), but is outside the 3- or 5-day period, then the security will not be reinstated in the index during the month. This means that any profit/loss resulting in a suspension for more than 3 or 5 days is not allowed for in the indices.

»Example

Consider a large non-government bond of appropriate maturity which is priced at 95 on Date *A* immediately prior to being suspended. On Date *B*, the bond is re-quoted at 80. What is the effect on the index?

Case	Suspension Date A	Re-quotation Date B	Effect
(i)	Monday 3rd	Friday 7th	Bond stays in index. Price drops from 95 to 80 on 7th.
ii)	Monday 29th	Friday 2nd	Bond remains in index until end of month at a price of 95, when it is removed.
(iii)	Monday 3rd	Friday 16th	Bond stays in index at a price of 95 until Monday 10th, when it is removed. It is not re-instated, and allowance is not made for all the price decrease.

The possibility of reinstating a bond which was temporarily suspended for over a week during a month was considered but rejected, since its treatment would depend on the suspension date in the month, and would involve re-calculating the index back to the suspension date.

Bonds in default

If a bond included in the index goes into default part-way through a month (the selection period), then two scenarios can occur:

i)   It can continue to be priced with two-way prices;

ii) It ceases to be priced, or two-way prices are no longer available.

In the former case, it is possible to continue to include the defaulted bond in a clean price index and the total return index, if the coupon is immediately set to zero. However, it has to be excluded from the calculations for average redemption yield, duration and average life, since any redemption date and value have become conjecture.

In the latter case, even the price indices cannot continue to include it, unless of course some assumption is made about the price. One can take two different views about the value of the bonds in default. These are:

- The default was expected and the last price of the bonds already discounted its effect;

- The bonds are now worthless.

Depending on the circumstances, either view could be correct although, in practice, the truth is likely often to lie between the two.

Recommendation ➤   As a result, it is recommended that as soon as the bond is known to have gone into default an attempt is made to get a price for it. This price is then included in the index calculation for one day. The bond is then removed from the index irrespective of whether a price continues to be quoted or not.

Needless to say, a bond in default should never be included in the index selection at the beginning of the month.

Partly-paid securities

Bonds are sometimes issued in partly-paid form, with the remainder being payable in one or more tranches on specified dates. For example, a bond could be issued at a price of 24 with a further 75 to pay in 9 months' time, instead of at an issue price of 99. If, during the period that the bond is partly-paid, interest rates move then the percentage price movement of the partly-paid security is likely to be much greater than that of an equivalent fully-paid bond.

Using the above example, if the price of an equivalent fully-paid bond moves from 99 to 103 as a result of interest rate changes, then the price of the partly-paid issue will probably increase from 24 to approximately 28. In percentage terms, this increase is about four times as great.

The question arises as to how one should treat such securities as they are much more volatile than equivalent fully-paid ones. Various options are possible.

i)   Treat as partly-paid, with the inherent greater volatility. When a call is due, finance it by selling appropriate numbers of securities in the index;

ii) Treat as partly-paid, but include the call money which is sitting on deposit;

iii) Treat as fully-paid, i.e. increase the quoted price by the sum of the future calls, accrue interest at the fully-paid rate and adjust the initial coupon payment appropriately, and give it the fully-paid weighting.

The *first* option caused a problem some years ago in the UK gilt-edged market where most of the new bonds in the 'over 15 years' category were issued in partly-paid form. As a result of interest rate changes, the index performed better than all the fund managers. This was in part caused by them setting aside funds for the future calls. (*see* Bibliography: *FT-Actuaries British Government Securities Indices* paper for more details).

The *second* option of including the call money—which is on deposit—is not satisfactory, since one has to specify and agree the interest accrued.

The *third* option has its attractions, since it reduces the volatility of the partly-paid securities, but it is only an approximation to reality. In effect, it assumes that the call money is on deposit at an interest rate which is close to, or equals, the coupon rate of the new issue.

The difference between the first and the third options can be illustrated by the example shown below.

»Example

Consider an index which consists of two securities, *A* and *B*, each with a nominal

Cont.

(cont.)

amount of 100. At the base date, *A* is fully-paid with a price of 100, and *B* is partly-paid with a price of 25. A future call of 75 is due on *B*. During the period being considered, the prices of *A* and *B* both rise by 10.

If option 1 is used, the new index value would be:

$$100 \times \frac{(110 \times 100 + 35 \times 100)}{(100 \times 100 + 25 \times 100)} = 100 \times \frac{145}{125} = 116$$

On the other hand, the option 3 approach gives:

$$100 \times \frac{(110 \times 100 + (35 + 75) \times 100)}{(100 \times 100 + (25 + 75) \times 100)} = 110$$

Recommendation ➤   It is recommended that the option 3 treatment is used, since this reflects the performance of a prudent investment manager, who has the funds for the future calls set aside. As will be seen, this agrees with the revised FT-Actuaries Index calculations.

Serial bond partial redemption

Some bonds are redeemed in several tranches in a predetermined way for each holder. e.g. 50 per cent is redeemed at 100 on 1/6/1993 and 50 per cent at 100 on 1/6/1994. Such bonds have been issued in the Dutch government bond market. When the holder knows in advance what proportion of the bonds will be redeemed at each date, it is called a serial bond.

A partial redemption of a serial bond can occur when it is in the index. When such a redemption occurs the price of the bond may move independently of any market changes. However, the investors as a whole should not profit or lose as a result of the partial redemption.

»Example

Consider a serial bond (see Figure 6) which is trading at 101 when 50 per cent is drawn at 100 per cent. If everything else remains the same, the price of the remaining security will jump to 102 per cent.

The value of the holding (net of accrued interest) does not change on the drawing date. Similarly, the values of any index containing the bond should not jump as a result of the drawing or the partial redemption.

In fact, if the index consisted of just this bond and at the original date it had an index value of 101, after the partial redemption it should still have a value of 101.

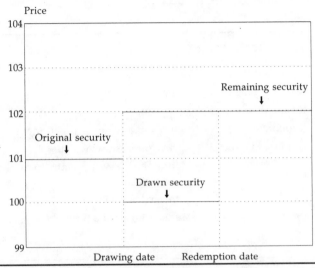

Figure 6   **Serial bond partial redemption**

It should be noted that it is conventional to value any drawn bonds at the called redemption price and ignore the value of money between the drawing date and redemption.

From the point of view of index calculations, ignoring the effect of partial redemptions is obviously unsatisfactory as illustrated above. When calculating the indices, it is possible to assume that the monies from the drawing are available for reinvestment on either the drawing or the redemption date.

The monies are, in practice, only available on the redemption date, but such an assumption requires a dummy security to be created. This security has a price of the redemption value and the coupon rate of the original bond.

If, on the other hand, it is assumed that the monies are immediately available, all that is required is to adjust the prices as illustrated above. This assumption can distort the calculation if the market moves between the call and redemption date, or if the security being drawn has a coupon rate which is different to the market average one.

Recommendation➤   On balance, it was felt that the complication of introducing a dummy called security more than compensated for the shortcomings of assuming the immediate availability of the monies.

This dummy security is introduced on the call date, and the amount in issue of the remaining security reduced appropriately.

»Dummy called security terms

Issue date:	drawing date
Redemption date:	all on the specified date
Redemption value:	as specified — frequently par
Coupon:	rates and payments as per original issue
Amount in issue:	prior to the drawing date = 0
	from the drawing date to redemption = amount called
	after redemption = 0
Price:	redemption value throughout

Bonds being called

Some bonds are callable by the issuer for early redemption on specific dates, or at any time between two dates, at prices which are frequently different to the normal redemption price on a certain number of days' notice. This notice period is frequently 30 or 90 days, although it may be less.

»Examples

■ Eutelsat 6½% Ecu bonds 1986-94

Callable on 20 days' notice from 12 May 1991 at 100.375, 1992 at 100.25, 1993 at 100.125

■ Euratom 10% Ecu bonds 1985-97

Callable as a whole or in part on coupon dates only on 30 days' notice from 22 March 1994 at 101.5, 1995 at 101 and 1996 at 100.5

As discussed earlier, if the yield on a bond to call is less than that to redemption, it is assumed that the bond will be called and its operative life adjusted appropriately.

If the prices of the bond move around par, then it is possible for its operative life to jump several times during the month.

If it is expected, at the index constituent review time, that because of a bond's price and yield it will be called in the near future, then it is un-likely—although possible—that the bond would be considered for selection as its calculated operative life will probably be less than one year.

»Example

■ UK Treasury 14% 1998-2001

This is callable in 1998 which is assumed to be the date for the operative redemp-tion as, in October 1993, it was yielding under 7 per cent.

It is possible for a bond in the index to be called. The issuer may wish to call the bond for a variety of reasons. For example, many bonds have a call option if the tax position changes.

»Example

Consider a 6 per cent annual bond with a final maturity date of 1 May 1998 which is callable on 30 days' notice on 1 April 1994 for redemption at par on 1 May 1994.

If the bond was priced at 99.999 per cent on 1 April 1994, it would be assumed that it would not be called whereas, if the price was 100.001 per cent, that it would be. The effect on the calculations is:

Price	Operative life	Duration	Redemption yield
99.999	4 years 30 days	3.55 years	c. 6.0%
100.001	30 days	30 days	c. 6.0%

Recommendation ➤   When a bond is called, although it is often possible to trade in the bond up to the call maturity date, they usually cease to be liquid. As a result the convention is immediately to set the price of the bond to its call price. In this way, the indices reflect the capital gain or loss that occurs as a result of the call. The bond is left in the index until either it is redeemed, or the constituents are reviewed at the end of the month, when it will be removed.

Bonds that have been called are excluded from the selection process.

Repurchase of the security by the issuer

The outstanding amount of an issue diminishes as a result of the issuer repurchasing bonds in the market. This could occur as the result of the exercise of a purchase fund, a sinking fund, or another reason.

The proposed formulae will satisfactorily accommodate the change in capital, although there are securities where such a purchase may effect the proposed amortization structure of the bond, and hence its average maturity[1]. The amount outstanding in the calculations should be reduced as soon as it is known. The security will normally remain in the basket until it is reviewed at the end of the month.

Takeover bid, public offer of exchange, etc.

In the case where a temporary suspension of trading occurs before the complete conditions of the deal are announced, the security is temporarily removed from the sample. It is reinstated as soon as the quotation is resumed when, theoretically, the price of the security incorporates the capital gains due to the operation and the changes due to the normal market movements.

At the end of the operation, if the security is replaced it should obviously be removed from the calculations. Similarly securities which are expected to be restructured in the next month should not be included in a new basket.

---

[1] Such securities are normally excluded from the calculations.

Chapter 7

Bond universe selection criteria

The universe of bonds considered for inclusion in the market indices is based on all 'normal' bonds in the sector, which do not have any special conditions attached to them, and reflect the nature of the market.

The basic principles used for deciding whether to include a bond or not in the index selection universe were:

- One should try to compare instruments like with like. For example, the expected redemption yield of a bullet bond is not directly comparable with that of a index-linked bond; however, it is still possible to compare historical price and total return performance.

- Future cashflows should be 'quantifiable', as in the case of a fixed-rate bullet bond which is not in default.

»Example

A floating-rate note (FRN) may have its coupon payments fixed relative to the London interbank offered rate (Libor). Although this means that comparison with other FRNs based on Libor are valid, comparisons with fixed-rate bonds are difficult.

The following conditions were considered for inclusion or exclusion of the bonds in the index universe.

The conclusions refer to whether the bonds should or not be included according to the EFFAS index rules, or whether such bonds could form a constituent part of indices which are directly comparable. It does not mean that such bonds cannot be included in indices which are calculated in a similar way, however the returns may not be strictly comparable.

»Example

It is perfectly reasonable to calculate a convertible bond index using the same formulae, but its performance will be related in part to the underlying equity market.

Recommendation ➤   It is recommended that any variations on the standard selections are explicitly stated.

1. Bonds with less than one year to final maturity

Bonds with under a year to final maturity tend either to be compared with money market instruments, or be illiquid.

Recommendation ➤   Such bonds are not to be included in the bond indices. A different approach to calculating money/cash market indices is discussed in Chapter 12.

2. Fixed-rate bullet bonds

Recommendation ➤   Fixed-rate bullet bonds should be included in the potential universe as the future cashflows are usually predictable, unless they are rejected for any other reason.

»Example

■ An example of where bullet bonds have been removed from the government bond universe is in Ireland where two bonds (Irish Capital 11¾% April 2000 and Irish Exchequer 8¼% October 2003) are not tradeable as they are held in very tight hands. In one case, a single holder accounts for 60 per cent of the issue.

Similarly, bullets with delayed, or broken, first coupon payments should also be included.

3. Zero-coupon bonds

The difference between normal and zero-coupon bonds is just that the latter only has one cashflow at redemption. Zero-coupon bonds can thus be included in the indices. However, when considering price indices as opposed to the total return, should one attempt to separate the price gain stemming from the accrued interest component as opposed to the market movement? It would be possible to make adjustments for a theoretical coupon and adjusted price, based on, say, the original issue yield. This approach is not recommended. Similarly, in some markets, zero-coupon bonds tend to have different yields to equivalent bullet bonds, due to the fact that no assumptions have to be made about the return on reinvesting coupons and that capital gains are often taxed differently to coupon payments. As a result, it may sometimes be desirable to treat them as a separate sub-index.

Recommendation ➤   Zero-coupon bonds may be included in the indices, or put into a separate sub-index.

4. Strips

In some markets, a few of the larger bonds have been stripped into their constituent individual cashflows (i.e. individual coupon payments and the redemption payment).

»Examples

■ Ecu 500m of the Republic of Italy 9¼%, 7 March 2011, was stripped into: Twenty Ecu 46.25m zero-coupon tranches redeemable at par on 7 March 1992, 1993, . . . 7 March 2011 and one zero-coupon tranche of Ecu 500m (principal) redeemable at par on 7 March 2011.

■ The Republic of France OAT 8.5% 25 April 2003 and 25 April 2023 French franc issues have both been stripped and the stripped coupon payments amalgamated. Similarly, the France OAT 8.5% 25 October 2008 and 25 October 2013 issues have also been stripped.

In effect, stripping a 5-year bond with an annual coupon creates 5 zero-coupon bonds, of which the final one is by far the largest as it includes the redemption value[1]. The stripped coupon payments may be amalgamated with other stripped bonds, as is the case with the French OAT example above.

---

[1] *The final payment is sometimes split into separate interest and capital payments because of different tax status. This is the situation with French OATs.*

Recommendation ➤   There is no reason why strips should not be included in any indices; however, care must be taken not to double count both the original bond and its stripped components.

It should be noted that, even for a large bond, the effect of stripping produces a number of very small issues, plus the much larger final payment. This means that the coupon strips are likely to be excluded from both the Tracker and Bellwether indices because of their size.

The relationship between the original bond and its constituents is often arbitraged. Should strips become expensive more will be created, whereas when strips are cheap they can be reconstituted into the original bond as happens in the US.

5. Irredeemable or undated bonds

Irredeemable or undated bonds are bonds without a final maturity date. There is, however, usually some sort of call or put option to enable the holder to get his capital back.

»Example

■ UK War Loan Sterling 3½% 1952 or after

It may be redeemed at the British government's option on 3 months' notice at par. Immediately after the Second World War, when interest rates were much lower, it was traded above par.

Recommendation ➤   Such bonds should thus either be put into a separate maturity band or included/excluded according to the treatment of the appropriate call or put option.

6. Graduated-rate securities

Graduated-rate securities are bonds where the coupon payments change in a predefined way over their life. Hence they normally have a fixed cashflow stream.

Recommendation ➤   They should be included in any index calculations.

»Example

■ European Coal & Steel Community US dollar graduated-rate bonds 1978-99

Cont.

(cont.)

The annual coupon was 9¾ per cent up to January 1984 and 9 per cent there-after.

---

7. Partly-paid securities

The future calls on the partly-paid securities are in effect negative coupon payments, hence they can be included. However, price movements on partly-paid securities as a proportion of their partly-paid price have greater volatility than fully-paid ones, with the result that index movements may be exaggerated.

Recommendation ➤   Treat such securities as if they were fully-paid (*see* Chapter 6, 'Treatment of events').

8. Floating-rate notes

Floating-rate notes (FRNs) tend to perform differently to fixed-rate bonds, due to the fact that as the coupons are frequently reset, the prices tend to stay close to par.

For floating-rate notes, it may be desirable to calculate an average current yield or discounted margin, as opposed to a gross redemption yield. Otherwise similar calculations can be made.

Recommendation ➤   It is recommended that FRNs are excluded from the normal bond indices. However, a separate index could be calculated for these instruments.

9. Index-linked bonds

Some bonds are issued with their coupons and/or redemption value indexed to the value of some external criteria or index.

»Example

■ The Lafarge Coppée French franc issue, where the redemption value is linked to the performance of the Lafarge Coppée equity stock between 1991 and 1994. In the Danish mortgage and the UK gilt-edged section, stocks have been issued where the coupons and the redemption value rise in line with the consumer or retail price indices.

The quoted returns on index-linked bonds, even when they form a homogenous group are not directly comparable with those on conventional bonds, as they appeal to different types of investors with different investment criteria.

»Example

■ In the UK gilt-edged market in October 1993, conventional bonds yielded between 5.30 per cent and 7.50 per cent, whereas the index-linked bonds gave a **real rate of return** of circa 3 per cent

---

Recommendation ➤   As a result, it is recommended that index-linked bonds are excluded from the indices. However, special indices may be calculated for a homogenous group of bonds which are linked to the same index.

10. Callable bonds

In some government bond markets (such as the UK and US), bonds which are callable form a significant section of the market. As a result it is desirable to include them in the indices. In other markets (e.g. for eurobonds), callable bonds are not significant, with a result that it is easier to exclude them and avoid some of the problems below.

If bonds which are callable by the issuer are included, the life of the bond is deemed to be that which gives the worst yield to the investor[1]. Once a callable bond is included in a maturity basket, it stays in the basket until the next selection—irrespective of the price movements and assumed operative life.

For a bond which is callable at par, the redemption yield to the call date when the price is just above par is not significantly different to the yield to the final maturity date when it is just below par. However, there is a jump in the expected life and duration of the bond between the two dates. This in turn has a non-continuous effect on the average index values for life, duration, convexity and redemption yield. It will be seen (in Chapter 8) that the average redemption yield will jump as it is calculated by averaging the in-

---

[1] *If the yield to call gives the worst yield to the investor, the issuer, other things being equal, may not call the bond since on an option adjusted spread (OAS) basis it may still be expensive.*

dividual redemption yields which have been weighted by duration and size of issue.

The effect of changing the expected operative life of callable bonds means that bonds selected to have one average life can have one that is completely different a few days later.

Another problem that can occur is that some bonds can actually be called after being selected for the index. An exclusion rule, such as one which precludes any bonds that can be called in the next year, is very restrictive and would probably remove too many securities unnecessarily (such as the UK War Loan 3% stock which has no final redemption date but, as it can be theoretically called at any time, would never be included. This is unlikely in the near future as the price is currently about £50).

Recommendation ➤   Exclude unless they form a significant proportion of the market sector.

11. Puttable bonds

Puttable bonds give the holder the right to sell the bonds back to the issuer at specified dates before the maturity date of the bond.

»Example

■ Belgium US dollar 9.2% 1990-2010.

Normally redeemable at par on 28 June 2010. However, there exists a holder's option on 30 days' notice to require early repayment of the principal on 28 June 2000 at 100.

It is possible to make the same assumptions as for callable bonds—i.e. that the holder will act in his own best interest. This results in the assumption that the bond put options will be exercised if the yield to put is greater than the yield to maturity[1]. Thus, until the end of the notice period for the first put option, it would be possible to include the bond in a similar way. However, now there is an added complication, since all the holders of the

---

[1] *In practice, whether the holder exercises the put option or not may be in part the result of an option adjusted spread (OAS) analysis, which allows for the shape of the yield curve.*

bonds are very unlikely to exercise their put option at the same date. In fact, in some cases, it may be advantageous for holders to take different actions according to their own tax positions. Often, residual amounts of nominal exist as some holders forget—or are unable to—exercise their option, or holders cannot be traced.

When the put option is partially exercised, there is often no statement as to how much of the bond is still in issue, with the result that its correct weight in the index cannot be determined. Similarly, it means that the average performance of all the holders of the issue cannot be determined.

Recommendation ➤   If put issues form a significant proportion of the market sector and information on the amount of the issue outstanding is available, as is the case with some government bonds, then there is no reason for excluding them. However, this is frequently not the case.

12. Extendible bonds

Recommendation ➤   Bonds are sometimes extendible at the holder's option. In effect, this is very similar to a put option and, as a result it is recommended that they are normally excluded.

»Example

■ State Bank of New South Wales US dollar extendible FRNs 1988-98

On the coupon date in February 1993, and every 5 years thereafter, holders have the option to extend the life of the Bonds by 10 years from the holder's option date. Noteholders who exercise their option to extend the maturity of their notes will on 16 February 1993 received a bonus of $275 per $10,000 of principal notes held.

---

13. Bonds with sinking funds

Bonds with sinking funds are deemed to be bonds where the issuer is required to buy back a proportion of the bonds either in the market, or by lot, at predefined dates prior to redemption. The holder of the bonds does not know if any of his bonds will be redeemed at a specific date or not. If the proportion of the bonds held to be redeemed can be determined prior to the date, they are regarded as serial bonds.

»Example

■ City of Copenhagen Danish kroner 8⅜% 23 May 1998

The sinking fund is satisfied by annual drawings from 23 May 1995 and will retire 75 per cent of the issue prior to maturity.

Recommendation ➤   Sinking fund bonds are usually excluded because of the unpredictability of the cashflows to the holder, and the lack of information on the amount outstanding.

14. Bonds with serial redemptions

Serial bonds in this context are defined to be bonds where the redemption schedule of a holding is known to the investor. As a result, there is no reason why they should not be included in any indices.

»Example

Until 1989, in the Netherlands, government bonds were frequently issued for redemption in tranches over several years. e.g.

■ Nederland 8% 1989-95/99

This security will be redeemed in five equal instalments on 1st October in the years 1995 to 1999. The bonds are redeemed by drawing about 2 weeks before the redemption date. Holders get the average proportional amount redeemed at each date, so they can predict their cashflows.

For the purpose of the index maturity sub-bands, a serial bond is classified as if it were to be totally redeemed on the non-discounted average redemption date.

»Example

A serial bond redeems 25 per cent of its capital on 30 June 1997 and the remaining 75 per cent on 30 June 2001.

The average redemption date for such a bond is 30 June 2000

Cont.

(cont.)

i.e. Average date $= \dfrac{25 \times (30 \text{ June } 1997) + 75 \times (30 \text{ June } 2001)}{100}$

On the other hand, it may be felt that a better measure of the life of a serial bond is equivalent life, i.e. the time to the discounted average re-demption date. This was rejected on the grounds that the equivalent life calculations are dependent on the price, and hence the yield, of the security. In fact, two securities with the same redemption schedules will have differ-ent lives if they have different yields. (*See* discussion on equivalent life in Chapter 5).

»Example

Two bonds *A* and *B* are both redeemed in two equal tranches one year apart. Bond *A* yields 5 per cent and bond *B* 10 per cent.

The average redemption date is in both cases obviously halfway between the two dates.

Assuming both bonds accrue interest on a 360-day year basis, the equivalent life date, which is x days before the average life date is calculated by solving:

$$50 \times (180 - x) = 50 \times \dfrac{(180 + x)}{(1 + \dfrac{y}{100})}$$

where y is the redemption yield

This gives for bond *A*, $x = 9.5$ days, and for bond *B*, $x = 20$ days, i.e. the equiva-lent life for bond *B* is more than 10 days shorter than that of bond *A*.

Recommendation ➤   Serial bonds may be included in the indices, within the maturity band of their average life.

15. Bonds with purchase funds

The existence of the purchase fund frequently does not affect the return to a long-term holder of the bonds. Hence, there is no reason why such bonds with purchase funds should not be included in any indices.

However, until about 10 years ago, French bonds were frequently issued with annual redemption instalments, which could be partly satisfied by the issuer buying back the bonds in the market below par. The redemption schedule was then rate-dependent, as was the average life, etc. It would thus be very difficult to include such bonds in an index, and is not recommended. For a complete discussion, refer to the studies by Albert Allanic (*see* Bibliography).

Recommendation ➤   Normally include bonds with purchase funds.

16. Convertibles into equities

Convertibles may give the holder the option to convert the convertible bond into a specified number of equity shares at specified dates.

»Example

■ Chubb Capital Corporation 6% Subordinated Convertible Notes 1991-98

The holder has the right to convert into Chubb Corporation common stock from 24 June 1991 to 15 May 1998 at $86 each.

The bond is callable on 30 days' notice from 15 May 1994 at a variety of prices.

In some cases, the rights to convert cease some time before the redemption date of the bond, after which date the remaining bonds become the normal straight type. Any outstanding bonds can then be considered for inclusion in the indices—or not—according to the normal criteria.

There are many variations to the terms of convertible bonds, including different conversion rates at different times and sometimes cash adjustments on conversion.

»Example

■ Phoenix International 6% 1998, where each bond of £10,000 is convertible into 64 bearer shares of Prima Immobiliaria SA. A cash adjustment of £2,994.69 will be paid on conversion.

Recommendation ➤   Prior to the last conversion date, it is recommended that convertible bonds are excluded from the indices since their performance is, in part, dependent on the performance of the underlying equity shares and frequently the amount converted at any date is not known, with the result that the bonds' weighting in the index is suspect.

If the amount converted at each date is known soon after the conversion, it is possible to construct a special index of convertibles using the same methodology, provided one only includes standard convertibles and removes them from the index on the last conversion date.

17. Convertibles into bonds

Sometimes bonds are issued which give the holder the right to convert into other bonds at predefined dates and rates.

»Example

■ The UK Government Treasury Convertible 10% 1991 gave the holder the following conversion options:

Either into:

■ Conversion 9½% 2001

at the rate of £100 nominal converts on:

12/7/87	to £102 nominal
12/1/88	to £101
12/7/88	to £100
12/1/89	to £99
12/7/89	to £98

or, into:

■ Conversion 9% 2011

at the rate of £100 nominal converts on:

12/7/87	to £105 nominal
12/1/88	to £103
12/7/88	to £101
12/1/89	to £99
12/7/89	to £97

Occasionally, bonds have been issued which are convertible into floating-rate notes.

Bonds which are convertible into other fixed-rate bonds are, in effect, similar to bonds with put or extendible options, although the option terms are more complicated.

The conversion is assumed to take place only if it is advantageous to the holder (i.e. the holder will get a greater yield to maturity). Such bonds could thus be included in the index, if the necessary programming was in place, and the amounts outstanding were known.

Recommendation ➤   Bonds convertible into other bonds should normally be excluded from the calculations.

18. Bonds with warrants attached

Like convertibles, bonds with warrants attached tend to perform more closely to that of the underlying securities than bonds without warrants. The bonds also tend to have very low coupons. As a result whilst the warrants are still attached they should not be included in the bond indices. In some markets (eurobonds, for example), the warrants are frequently detached soon after issue. When this happens, the ex-warrant bonds can be considered for inclusion in the normal way. The performance of the detached bond warrants tends to mirror that of the underlying instrument. However, the percentage movements are usually much greater.

Recommendation ➤   Exclude bonds with warrants attached

19. Mortgage or asset-backed securities

Recommendation ➤   The redemption schedule associated with a mortgage or asset-backed security is frequently only an anticipated best guess. Thus, like sinking fund bonds, such securities should be excluded from the indices. However, if there are sufficient bonds which redeem in the same way, it may be possible to construct an index of their own, based on an anticipated repayment model.

20. Dual-currency bonds

Dual-currency bonds are securities where either the issuer or the holder may elect to pay/receive coupon and/or redemption payments in more than one currency, or where the coupon and redemption payments are in different currencies.

Recommendation ➤   Dual-currency bonds should be excluded, since the return to the holder is dependent on unpredictable external currency movements.

In addition, if one compares dual-currency bonds between the same two currencies, one frequently finds that the fixed-exchange rates and dates are different.

»Examples

■ Japanese yen/US dollar dual-currency bonds

Coupons in yen, redeemed in US dollars	Fixed conversion rate at redemption
American Express Credit 8% 4 September 1995	$4,808 = ¥ 1m
Banque Nationale de Paris 7% 29 November 1995	$1= ¥ 134.949998
Electricité de France 8% 31 October 1995	$5,434 = ¥ 1m

---

21. Securities with different tax status

If some securities in the sample have a different tax status, investors will take this into account and so they may perform differently.

»Examples

Examples of different tax treatment are:

■ Austrian government bonds issued prior to 1984, which are now subject to a 22 per cent withholding tax.

■ Some Italian bonds issued by the government and supranational organizations which are free of withholding tax, whereas the others are not.

■ UK gilt-edged FOTRA (Free of Tax to Residents Abroad) bonds.

■ Preference shares, which are often treated differently to corporate loan stocks.

Recommendation ➤   As a result, it is recommended that bonds with different tax status are normally excluded, however, it may be appropriate to include them in their own index.

The UK gilt-edged FOTRA bonds are an exception to this rule and are included in the UK indices. This is because the different tax status only applies to part of the market (i.e. not at all to UK investors), and partly as a result any difference in return is marginal.

22. Bonds with other special privileges

Recommendation ➤   These should be excluded, unless several bonds have the same special privilege which effects them in a comparable way, in which case a separate index can be constructed for them.

23. Private placements

Recommendation ➤   Except in the case of Swiss private placements, which are regarded as public issues, it is normal to exclude private placements from indices. This is because reliable market prices are not generally available, and prices are frequently calculated according to a matrix algorithm, or from a theoretical redemption yield curve. Both of these methods defeat the object of the index.

24. Very small or illiquid bonds

Recommendation ➤   Very small or illiquid bonds should be excluded, since a single transaction can have a considerable effect on the price. In addition, two-way prices frequently do not exist on a regular basis for such securities. Even when two-way prices do exist, the spread between the bid and the offer quotations is often very large, which does not inspire confidence in the calculated middle market price.

Very small and illiquid bonds will, in any case, be automatically excluded from the Tracker and Bellwether indices.

Note that such very small issues can occur as the result of a conversion offer for the original stock.

Bond selection summary table

	Bond Feature	Normal Treatment*
1	Bond with less than 1 year to final maturity	Exclude
2	Fixed-rate bullet bonds	Include
3	Zero-coupon bonds	Include
4	Strips	Include
5	Irredeemable bonds	Treat as a separate maturity band
6	Graduated-rate securities	Include
7	Partly-paid securities	Treat as fully-paid
8	Floating-rate notes	Exclude
9	Index-linked bonds	Exclude
10	Callable bonds	Exclude unless a significant proportion of the market sector
11	Puttable bonds	Exclude
12	Extendible bonds	Exclude
13	Bonds with sinking funds	Exclude
14	Bond with serial redemptions	Include
15	Bonds with purchase funds	Normally include
16	Convertibles into equities	Exclude
17	Convertibles in bonds	Exclude
18	Bonds with warrants attached	Exclude
19	Mortgage or asset-backed securities	Exclude
20	Dual-currency bonds	Exclude
21	Securities with different tax status	Normally exclude
22	Bonds with other special privileges	Exclude
23	Private placements	Normally exclude
24	Very small or illiquid bonds	Exclude

*This treatment may always be overridden in specific circumstances, provided this is stated and justified. If sufficient securities exist with the same feature, it may be desirable to construct a special index for them.

Chapter 8

Formulae

This section describes the recommended formulae for calculating the indices and associated values. The same formulae may be applied to maturity sub-groups, or the total market for All-bond, Tracker and Bellwether bond indices.

The formulae assume that the user can calculate the redemption yield, life, duration and convexity of a bond. A useful source for such calculations is the ISMA publication *Formulae for Yield and Other Calculations*.

The following types of information may be derived:

■ Indices

   Clean price index
   Gross price index
   Total return index
   Interest paid this year (reset to 0 on 1st January)

■ Average values

   Average coupon
   Average life
   Average duration
   Average convexity
   Average redemption yield
   Average current yield

The calculations below use the following notations:

Z_t value of criterion Z at time t
Z_{t-1} value of criterion Z at time $(t-1)$
Z_0 initial value of criterion Z
$Z_{i,t}$ value of criterion Z for the ith security at time t

P	clean price of the bond (i.e. without accrued interest). In markets where bid and offered prices are quoted, a middle price is used.
$P_{i,t}$	clean price of the ith bond at time t
$P*_{i,t}$	clean price of the ith bond at time t, adjusted on the call date only, for any partial serial redemptions. (see below). At all other times, it is the same as the unadjusted price P
A	accrued interest to the 'normal' settlement date
N	nominal value of amount outstanding if known, otherwise the issued amount
Y	redemption yield to assumed maturity date
L	life to assumed maturity date
D	duration
X	convexity
C	coupon rate per cent
$G_{i,t}$	value of any coupon payment received from the ith bond for 'normal' settlement at time t or since time $(t-1)$. If none the value $= 0$
R	redemption price of the bond

Treatment of a partial redemption

When a serial bond is partly redeemed, the price of the bond may jump as a result of the remaining securities being quoted ex the partial redemption.

The convention in the market-place is to assume that the part of the bond called for redemption, which is normally no longer tradeable, is now worth the redemption price, although this may not be received for some weeks. On the premise that the investor should not gain or lose money as a result of a partial redemption, it can be seen that, on a drawing date, the quoted price of the remaining securities should theoretically jump according to the following formula:

$$P*_t \times (N_t + NC_t) = P_t \times N_t + R_t \times NC_t$$

where,

t	time of the drawing
N_t	amount in issue outstanding after the drawing
NC_t	amount called for redemption in the drawing
R_t	redemption price of the bonds being called at time t
$P*_t$	price of the bonds immediately before the drawing
P_t	theoretical price of the remaining bonds after the drawing

In the above formula, the number of bonds in issue on the day prior to the drawing N_{t-1} will be the same as $(N_t + NC_t)$.

Please note that when there is a partial redemption, for the following formulae to work, a dummy security needs to be created between the drawing and partial redemption dates. (*See* relevant section in Chapter 6, 'Treatment of Events')

THE FORMULAE

The formulae are calculated as below. In all the calculations, the summations are over all securities that match the selection criteria at time t, and include any temporary dummy securities which have been created as a result of a partial redemption call.

Clean price index (*PI*)

$$PI_0 = 100$$

$$PI_t = PI_{t-1} \times \frac{\sum\limits_i P*_{i,t} \times N_{i,t-1}}{\sum\limits_i P_{i,t-1} \times N_{i,t-1}}$$

where the summations are over the bonds currently in the index.

Gross price index (*GI*)

The accrued interest (*AI*) in the gross price index is given by:

$$AI_t = \frac{\sum\limits_i A_{i,t} \times N_{i,t-1}}{\sum\limits_i P*_{i,t} \times N_{i,t-1}}$$

where the summations are over the bonds currently in the index.

The gross price index (*GI*) is then:

$$GI_t = PI_t \times (1 + AI_t)$$

It will be seen that the gross price index is derived from the clean price index as opposed to the other way round, which superficially may appear to be logical since an investor has to pay the gross price when purchasing a security. However, since the constituents of the index are reset on a monthly basis, when the accrued content of the index can jump, any clean price index which is derived from a gross price index would also jump in a way that is not justified by any price movement. It does, however, mean that the gross price index may jump at the month end.

»Example

Consider the example in the table below at the end of November when as a result of the different index constituents the average accrued interest drops from about 4 to 2 per cent. It can be seen that the calculated gross price index drops by over 1 point when the underlying clean price index rises.

Date	Clean price index (PI)	Accrued interest (AI × 100)	Gross price index (GI)
29/11	101.00	4.00	105.04
30/11	102.00	4.02	106.10
1/12	103.00	2.00	105.06
2/12	102.00	2.02	104.06

N.B. In this case, the drop in accrued interest does not imply that any interest has been paid.

Total return index (TR)

For a market where securities do not go XD (such as eurobonds), the total return index is calculated as follows:

$$TR_0 = 100$$

$$TR_t = TR_{t-1} \times \frac{\sum_i (P*_{i,t} + A_{i,t} + G_{i,t}) \times N_{i,t-1}}{\sum_i (P_{i,t-1} + A_{i,t-1}) \times N_{i,t-1}}$$

where the summations are over all the bonds currently in the index.

For markets where securities may be quoted XD the formulae are modified as overleaf:

$$TR_0 = 100$$

$$TR_t = TR_{t-1} \times \frac{\sum_i (P*_{i,t} + A_{i,t} + CP_{i,t} + G_{i,t}) \times N_{i,t-1}}{\sum_i (P_{i,t-1} + A_{i,t-1} + CP_{i,t-1}) \times N_{i,t-1}}$$

where the summations are over all the bonds currently in the index, and where CP is an amount that compensates if necessary for the quoted price not including the next coupon payment.

If the price at time t includes the next coupon payment then $CP_t = 0$. If the price at time t is ex the next coupon then CP_t is the next coupon payment.

»Example

A theoretical 9 per cent bond pays its annual coupon on 16th January, which is assumed to be a Saturday. The price of the bond is quoted XD for normal settlement from the 11th January. Assuming the bond accrues interest on a 360-day year, we have:

Settlement	Fri 8 Jan	Mon 11 Jan	Fri 15 Jan	Sat 16 Jan	Mon 18 Jan	Tue 19 Jan
Price status	Cum	Ex	Ex	Payment	Cum	Cum
Accrued A_t	8.800	-0.125	-0.025	-	0.050	0.075
	(352 days)	(-5 days)	(-1 day)	-	(2 days)	(3 days)
CP_t	0	9.000	9.000	-	0	0
CP_{t-1}	0	0	9.000	-	9.000*	0
G_t	0	0	0	-	9.000	0
$A_t + CP_t + G_t$	8.800	8.875	8.975	-	9.050	0.075

*the price was still XD on the previous calculation day (15th January)

Note: A security is not regarded as XD on a coupon date, when the accrued is zero.

Interest paid this year (IN)

The interest paid this year calculation gives the accumulated income expressed as a percentage of the gross price index. It is reset to zero at the beginning of each year. The interest paid calculation enables a total return index to be calculated for portfolios subject to tax on income received.

$IN_{ts} = 0$ where ts = the time at the beginning of each calendar year

$$IN_t = IN_{t-1} + GI_{t-1} \times \frac{\sum_i G_{i,t} \times N_{i,t-1}}{\sum_i (P_{i,t-1} + A_{i,t-1}) \times N_{i,t-1}}$$

where the summations are over all the bonds currently in the index.

Average coupon (CO)

The average coupon (CO) is given by:

$$CO_t = \frac{\sum_i C_{i,t} \times N_{i,t}}{\sum_i N_{i,t}}$$

where the summations are over all the bonds currently in the index.

For this calculation, the securities are weighted by the amount outstanding, as the prices are not relevant.

Average life (LF)

When looking at the bonds considered to be within a maturity band, it was felt that the measure of life for serial bonds should be the average life and not the equivalent life, as the latter varies with the price of the bond.

The group average life calculation used should produce the same results for a serial bond, irrespective of whether it is treated as a single security, or as several separate bullet bonds with size and maturity dates reflecting the partial redemptions. This criterion is again satisfied by using the crude average life calculation, as opposed to the equivalent life.

The average life (LF) for the index is given by:

$$LF_t = \frac{\sum_i L_{i,t} \times N_{i,t}}{\sum_i N_{i,t}}$$

where the summations are over all the bonds currently in the index.

Average duration (DU)

Calculating an average duration for all the future cashflows of the constituents of an index would be a large task, hence an approximation based on creating a weighted average of the individual bond durations is deemed desirable.

Various weights including the nominal value and market value of the bonds were considered. It was decided that market value was the preferred choice since, in the special case where all the bonds yield the same amount (the index yield), it produces the same value as the true duration.

»Example

Consider an index consisting of two zero-coupon securities, X and Y. The portfolio holds a nominal amount of N_x in security X and N_y in security Y.

Security X is redeemed at par in L_x years and, similarly, Y is redeemed in L_y years.

Since both securities do not pay any coupon, their durations are the same as their lives.

i.e. $D_x = L_x$

$D_y = L_y$

where,

D_n = duration of security n

If both securities yield the same, this is also the yield of the portfolio and hence the duration of the portfolio D_p is given by:

$$D_p = \frac{N_x \times L_x \times v^{L_x} + N_y \times L_y \times v^{L_y}}{N_x \times v^{L_x} + N_y \times v^{L_y}}$$

where,

v annualized discounting factor

i.e. if the annualized yield is y, then $v = \dfrac{1}{(1 + y)}$

($y = 0.08$ for a yield of 8%)

Now the current market value of the holding in security X is just the present value of the repayment discounted by the redemption yield rate y. That is, it is given by:

$M_x = N_x \times v^{L_x}$

Cont.

(cont.)

Similarly,

$M_y = N_y \times v^{L_y}$ where,

M_n = current market value of security n

Thus, the formula above for the portfolio duration D_p can be re-written:

$$D_p = \frac{D_x \times M_x + D_y \times M_y}{M_x + M_y}$$

i.e. the portfolio duration is just the average duration of the securities weighted by their current market values.

This logic can easily be extended to any portfolio provided all the constituents yield the same.

The average duration (*DU*) for the index is given by:

$$DU_t = \frac{\displaystyle\sum_i D_{i,t} \times (P_{i,t} + A_{i,t}) \times N_{i,t}}{\displaystyle\sum_i (P_{i,t} + A_{i,t}) \times N_{i,t}}$$

where the summations are over all the bonds currently in the index.

Average convexity (CX)

In a similar way to duration, the average convexity of an index is calculated by averaging the convexities of the constituent bonds weighted by their market values. It can be proved that, if all the securities yield the same, then this is mathematically correct.

The average convexity (CX) for the index is given by:

$$CX_t = \frac{\displaystyle\sum_i X_{i,t} \times (P_{i,t} + A_{i,t}) \times N_{i,t}}{\displaystyle\sum_i (P_{i,t} + A_{i,t}) \times N_{i,t}}$$

where the summations are over all the bonds currently in the index.

Average gross redemption yield (RY)

The formula used for calculating the average redemption yield of an index needs some explanation, as it is not immediately obvious.

For example, consider a portfolio which consists of $1,000,000 worth of stock in each of two securities. Both of these securities have a 10 per cent coupon. One of them has a life to maturity of one week and a redemption yield of 20 per cent, whereas the other one has a life of 10 years and one week and a redemption yield of 10 per cent. *What is the average redemption yield of the portfolio?*

Although both holdings have a very similar value, the redemption yield of the portfolio is patently not $(10 + 20)/2 = 15$ per cent as this would imply that the portfolio manager was expecting to reinvest the proceeds of the first stock to yield 20 per cent in one week's time. In fact, it must be very close to 10 per cent, as the second stock has a life which is more than 500 times longer than the first.

To calculate the true redemption yield of all the cashflows in the index would be a very laborious operation. However, it is found that a good approximation to the yield can be obtained by weighting the individual bond yields by the size of the holding multiplied by its duration, since duration is just the discounted life of all the future cashflows of the bond. That is, we have:

$$RY_t = \frac{\sum_i Y_{i,t} \times D_{i,t} \times (P_{i,t} + A_{i,t}) \times N_{i,t}}{\sum_i D_{i,t} \times (P_{i,t} + A_{i,t}) \times N_{i,t}}$$

where the summations are over the bonds currently in the index.

It is normal to display average yields for an index compounded according to the conventions of the market (e.g. compounded semi-annually in the UK and USA, and annually in France and the eurobond markets). However, if cross-country comparisons are being made yields compounded annually are recommended.

»Formula — Yield compounding frequency adjustment

A semi-annual redemption yield Y_s may be converted to an annual redemption yield Y_a, and vice versa, by applying the formula:

Cont.

(cont.)

$$\left(1 + \frac{Y_a}{100}\right) = \left(1 + \frac{Y_s}{200}\right)^2$$

This formula is independent of the coupon payment frequency of the bond, and its method of accruing interest.

»Example

A semi annual yield of 10 per cent is equivalent to an annual yield Y_a given by:

$$Y_a = 100\left\{1 + \frac{10}{200}\right\}^2 - 100$$

$$= 10.25\%$$

Average current yield (CY)

The current yield of a bond is also known as a flat, running, or interest yield. By convention in the market-place, it is defined to be the coupon C of a bond divided by its clean price P.
    The average current yield (CY) is given by:

$$CY_t = 100 \times \frac{\sum\limits_{i} C_{i,t} \times N_{i,t}}{\sum\limits_{i} P_{i,t} \times N_{i,t}}$$

where the summations are over the bonds currently in the index.

Chapter 9

Nature of the calculations

The methodology described consists of selecting the constituents of an index at the end of each month and keeping the same constituents throughout the following month. However, the methodology would still work if the selection period was changed.

The calculations themselves imply that jumps in values, which are not associated with price movements, occur under predefined circumstances, and are often restricted to being at the end of a month.

Constituent changes during the month

It is possible for the constituents of an index to change during the month. This can occur if:

- an issue goes into default;

- a price is not received for a security for more than 3 business days (for government indices), or 5 business days otherwise. In this case, the bond is removed and not reinstated in the index during the month, even if prices are again available;

- an index constituent bond becomes fungible with another one during the month. It is possible for the original index bond to disappear and be replaced by the new bond. However, in this case, the index values should not jump;

- a dummy bond is created as a result of a partial redemption drawing.

Index calculations

The index calculations have been designed so that the clean price and total return indices should be continuous both during, and at the end of, each month—with jumps being related to the price movements of their constituents.

For example, the price movement in both calculations is based on the price movements of today's constituents from the previous day. Similarly, the payment of a coupon should not cause a jump in the total return index.

On the other hand, the gross price index may have discontinuities caused by a variety of reasons, which include:

- When a bond pays interest, or starts to be quoted ex-coupon, the effect of that payment will cause a drop in the average accrued interest in the sample, and hence a drop in the gross price index.

- At the end of a month the constituents of the index may change, with the result that the average accrued interest changes.

- Whenever the amount in issue of a bond changes, this will normally change the average accrued interest.

If none of the events described above occur, one would expect the gross price index to increase relative to the clean price index by an amount proportional to the increase of accrued interest at the average coupon rate over the relevant number of days.

The difference between the gross and the clean price index (*see* Figure 7) reflects the amount of accrued interest in the index. The difference will in-

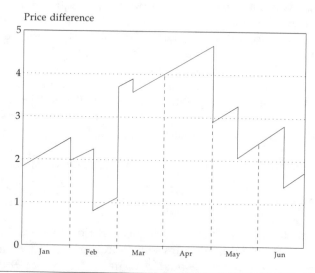

Figure 7   **Typical gross minus clean price index**

crease during the month at a rate which reflects the average coupon rate of the constituent bonds. It will drop whenever a bond pays a coupon. At the end of a month whenever the constituents change the clean price index is continuous, but the gross price index jumps to reflect the new accrued amount.

Average coupon

The average coupon of an index during the month will be flat unless, either the constituents of the index change (*see* 'Constituent changes during the month', above) or the amount in issue of a constituent changes. Such a change may occur if:

- a new tranche of a bond which is fungible with a constituent bond is issued;

- a constituent bond becomes fungible with another issue;

- a bond is partially redeemed.

At the end of a month, the average coupon may jump as the constituents may change.

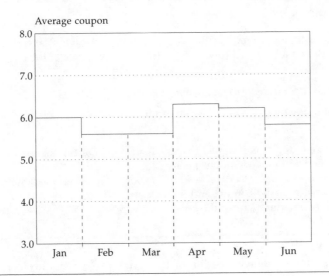

Figure 8   Typical index average coupon

Figure 8 shows a typical average coupon graph. It can be seen that during the month the value of the average coupon normally remains constant as the constituents of the index do not change. The change at the end of January in the graph could be caused by either a bond with a coupon of over 6 per cent being removed or a new one with a coupon of less than 6 per cent being included, or a combination of events.

The lack of any changes between February and March would occur if there are no alterations in the index constituents.

Average life

The average life of an index will normally reduce gradually over the month so that, at the end of the month, it is one month less than at the beginning. However, the average life may jump at the end of a month when the constituents change, or sometimes during the month if:

- the constituents change (see above);

- the amounts in issue change (see average coupon);

- the assumed operative life of a callable or puttable bond changes.

»Example

If a bond will be redeemed at 100 on 1 July 1999, unless it is called by the issuer for redemption at 100 on 1 July 1995, then the operative life of the bond is:

- to 1 July 1995 if the price is greater than 100
- to 1 July 1999 if the price is less than 100

(If the price is 100, it is assumed that the issuer will not call the bond). When the price of the bond moves from just below 100 to just above 100, there is no significant effect on the indices or the yield of the bond. However, the bond's operative life and duration will jump and so will the average index yield, as this is weighted by the durations of the constituent bonds.

Figure 9 shows the average life of the index progressively decreasing by one month during the month as the constituents do not change. At the end of the month, the average life may jump in either direction due to changes in the composition of the index. The lack of a jump between February and march could be caused by unchanged constituents.

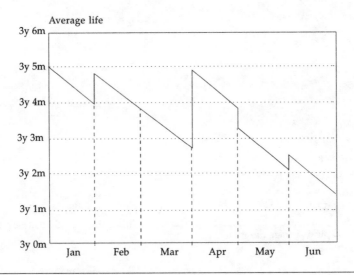

Figure 9   Typical average life

Average duration

The average duration of an index (*see* Figure 10) will tend to decrease gradually over the month if there are no jumps in the average life (see above) and if:

- the overall average group yield remains constant;

and

- no bond pays a coupon during the month.

Whenever a bond pays a coupon, its duration increases with a corresponding effect on the average group value.

Jumps may also occur during the month for the same reasons as average life, and at the end of a month when the constituents change.

If the average yield of an index does not change, then its average duration will tend to decrease at a rate of one month for one month elapsed. However, whenever one of the constituents pays a dividend, it will jump upwards. Jumps can occur in either direction at the end of the months, due to changes in the bonds.

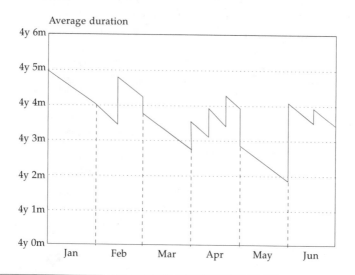

Figure 10   Typical average duration

Average gross redemption yield

The average gross redemption yield of an index during the month, which should track the yield of the market sector, will normally rise when the clean price index falls, and fall when the index rises. However, jumps may occur whenever the constituents of the index change, or whenever the duration of a constituent bond jumps for any reason. This is because the average group value is the average redemption yield of each bond, weighted by the product of its current market value and its duration.

Chapter 10

Creating composite indices

There is sometimes a requirement to construct a bond index of securities with a maturity expectation range that is greater than one already calculated. For example, there are Bloomberg/EFFAS government indices for maturity ranges of 1-3 years and 3-5 years, but not for 1-5 years. There are two possible ways of creating a 1-5 year index. The first is to calculate the new index from basic principles. This is often not an option since, apart from it taking a lot of computing and manpower, the basic data is often no longer available. The alternative is to combine the 1-3 year and 3-5 year indices together to get a good approximation to the 1-5 year index. A method of doing this is described below.

The proposed method can be used for combining both All-bond and Tracker indices. It is not suggested that one should combine Bellwether indices because of the sizes of the samples.

For both the All-bond and the Tracker calculations, the sub-indices are weighted together according to the relative size of *all* the potential securities in the sub-group, i.e. the weights for combining the Tracker indices are like the All-bond indices, the combined nominal or market value of all the bonds that were eligible for inclusion in the All-bond sub-index.

Please note that the weights used when combining together Tracker sub-indices are those for the equivalent All-bond sub-indices, if they are available. This is because the value of the constituents in a Tracker index may represent anything between 25 and 100 per cent of the index group, with the result that the individual groups could be under- or over-represented. Using the All-bond sub-index weights does not guarantee that the correct weights are applied, but it should be normally more accurate.

In order to calculate the combined index, it is necessary to derive the weights S and W, as below:

$$S_{I,t} = \sum_{i \in I} N_{i,t}$$

Cont.

(cont.)

$$WI_{I,t} = \sum_{i \in I} P_{i,t} \times N_{i,t}$$

where,

$S_{I,t}$ nominal weight of sub-group I at time t
$W_{I,t}$ market weight of sub-group I at time t
$P_{i,t}$ price of the ith security at time t
$N_{i,t}$ outstanding amount in issue of the ith security at time t
and where the summation is over all the potential components of sub-group i.

The indices and associated averages are then calculated as follows:

Clean price index (PI)

The clean price index for sub-group $(1 + 2)$ can be derived from indices for sub-groups 1 and 2 as follows:

$$PI_{1+2,0} = 100$$

$$PI_{1+2,t} = PI_{1+2,t-1} \times \frac{W_{1,t} \times \dfrac{PI_{1,t}}{PI_{1,t-1}} + W_{2,t} \times \dfrac{PI_{2,t}}{PI_{2,t-1}}}{W_{1,t} + W_{2,t}}$$

where,

$PI_{g,t}$ clean price index of sub-group g at time t
$W_{g,t}$ market weight of sub-group g at time t

Gross price index (GI)

$$GI_{1+2,t} = PI_{1+2,t} \times \frac{W_{1,t} \times \dfrac{GI_{1,t}}{PI_{1,t}} + W_{2,t} \times \dfrac{GI_{2,t}}{PI_{2,t}}}{W_{1,t} + W_{2,t}}$$

where,

$GI_{g,t}$ gross price index of sub-group g at time t

Total return index (*TR*)

$$TR_{1+2,0} = 100$$

$$TR_{1+2,t} = TR_{1+2,t-1} \times \frac{W_{1,t} \times \dfrac{TR_{1,t}}{TR_{1,t-1}} + W_{2,t} \times \dfrac{TR_{2,t}}{TR_{2,t-1}}}{W_{1,t} + W_{2,t}}$$

where,

$TR_{g,t}$ total return index of sub-group g at time t

Interest paid this year (*IN*)

$$IN_{1+2,t} = \frac{W_{1,t} \times IN_{1,t} + W_{2,t} \times IN_{2,t}}{W_{1,t} + W_{2,t}}$$

where,

$IN_{g,t}$ interest paid this year of sub-group g at time t

Average coupon (*CP*)

$$CP_{1+2,t} = \frac{S_{1,t} \times CP_{1,t} + S_{2,t} \times CP_{2,t}}{S_{1,t} + S_{2,t}}$$

where,

$CP_{g,t}$ average coupon of sub-group g at time t
$S_{g,t}$ nominal weight of sub-group g at time t

Average life (*LF*)

$$LF_{1+2,t} = \frac{S_{1,t} \times LF_{1,t} + S_{2,t} \times LF_{2,t}}{S_{1,t} + S_{2,t}}$$

where,

$LF_{g,t}$ average life of sub-group g at time t

Average duration (DU)

$$DU_{1+2,t} = \frac{W_{1,t} \times DU_{1,t} + W_{2,t} \times DU_{2,t}}{W_{1,t} + W_{2,t}}$$

where,

$DU_{g,t}$ average duration of sub-group g at time t

Average convexity (CX)

$$CX_{1+2,t} = \frac{W_{1,t} \times CX_{1,t} + W_{2,t} \times CX_{2,t}}{W_{1,t} + W_{2,t}}$$

where,

$CX_{g,t}$ average convexity of sub-group g at time t

Average redemption yield (RY)

$$RY_{1+2,t} = \frac{W_{1,t} \times RY_{1,t} \times DU_{1,t} + W_{2,t} \times RY_{2,t} \times DU_{2,t}}{W_{1,t} \times DU_{1,t} + W_{2,t} \times DU_{2,t}}$$

where,

$RY_{g,t}$ gross redemption yield of sub-group g at time t
$DU_{g,t}$ average duration of sub-group g at time t

Average current yield (CY)

$$CY_{1+2,t} = \frac{W_{1,t} \times CY_{1,t} + W_{2,t} \times CY_{2,t}}{W_{1,t} + W_{2,t}}$$

where,

$CY_{g,t}$ average current yield of sub-group g at time t

This formula is not strictly correct, since the average current yield is based on clean, as opposed to gross (clean plus accrued), prices. In practice, the difference is probably not significant.

Although this section describes how two maturity subsections of the same selection group may be combined together to form a larger maturity group, it does not address the problem of how to combine together indices from 2 different markets. For example, how do you create a bond index of UK and French government bonds? Apart from the problems of converting to a common currency, the problem arises as to what weights one should give the two different sets of indices. Possible weights might include weighted by gross domestic product of the two countries, weighted by size of the two bond markets, weighted by average market turnover, or even given equal weights. For more information, see the global index discussion in Chapter 15.

Chapter 11

Miscellaneous considerations

Allowing for tax

The calculations described so far have not considered the effect of any withholding or other tax on the investor. It is reasonably easy to approximate to the return an investor would get after allowing for both income and capital gains tax. It is conventional to assume that all taxes are payable on the coupon, redemption or realization dates, and not some time later. Conversely, if a coupon is subject to a reclaimable withholding tax, it is normal to assume the repayment is immediate.

In a market where income tax is chargeable on an accrual basis, such as the UK, a net total return index after income tax can be derived as below, since the total return index is made up of a capital component plus an income one.

This can be stated as:

$$dNTR_{1,2} = dPI_{1,2} + (dTR_{1,2} - dPI_{1,2}) \times (1 - tx)$$

where,

$dNTR_{1,2}$ percentage change in the net total return index between times 1 and 2

$dPI_{1,2}$ percentage change in the clean price index between times 1 and 2

$dTR_{1,2}$ percentage change in the gross total return index between times 1 and 2

tx tax rate (e.g. $tx = 0.4$ for a tax rate of 40%)

This formula works reasonably well if the period being considered is fairly short.

»Example

If an investor is subject to tax at 30 per cent on income and the total return and the clean price indices at times t_1 and t_2 are:

	t_1	t_2
Total return index *(TR)*	150	174
Clean price index *(PI)*	100	105

The percentage change $dTR_{1,2}$ in TR between t_1 and t_2 is:

$$dTR_{1,2} = \frac{(174 - 150)}{150} \times 100 = 16$$

and the percentage change $dPI_{1,2}$ in PI between t_1 and t_2 is:

$$dPI_{1,2} = \frac{(105 - 100)}{100} \times 100 = 5$$

Hence, the net after tax return $dNTR_{1,2}$ between the two dates is:

$$dNTR_{1,2} = 5 + (16 - 5) \times (1 - 0.3)$$

$$= 5 + 7.7$$

$$= 12.7$$

Similar adjustments should be made if the investor is subject to capital gains tax.

In some markets, the purchaser of a bond is taxed on the total coupon received, not just the accrued amount during the period of the investment. The effect of this is to cause the price of bonds to jump when they go ex-coupon.

»Example

Consider a bond which pays an annual 8 per cent coupon in a market which taxes income on average at $12\frac{1}{2}$ per cent, and the purchaser pays all the tax on the coupon.

Let us assume that the price of the bond immediately before going ex-coupon on the coupon date is 95 per cent, then the gross price of the bond is:

95 + a coupon of 8 per cent.

Cont.

the market assesses an average tax liability of 8 x .125 = 1 per cent on
ut.

On the coupon date, the price of the bond will rise to compensate for the reduced tax liability as the accrued interest is now 0. Thus, the clean price of the
bond will jump 1 per cent to compensate.

Some practical considerations

When the indices were first calculated, some practical problems arose. In
hindsight, it was clear that allowance should have been made for the following:

- One of the criteria used for the Tracker index for identifying the
  quality of the prices was the average spread between bid and offered prices. In the summer of 1992, after the Danish vote on Maas-
  tricht, all the price spreads in Portuguese escudo and Spanish
  peseta eurobonds widened considerably, with the result that the
  number of bonds initially selected for the following month was
  considerably reduced.

- The US dollar eurobond Tracker index with a 1-5 year maturity
  band was dominated, in 1992, by very large Japanese ex-warrant
  stocks. These stocks had very low coupons, and were relatively illiquid. As a result, they in no way represented the trading and performance in this area. In this case, it was possible to remove them
  by demanding a higher quality of prices, but it is a situation which
  could occur elsewhere.

- It is desirable to consider only homogeneous groups of bonds. For
  example, in the compilation of the eurobond Swiss franc Tracker
  index, one bond was selected which had a yield three times as great
  as the rest. This distorted the calculations and increased the average
  yield by about 1 per cent.

- It is not practical to calculate an All-bond index in markets where
  large number of bonds are not tradeable. Such bonds either depress
  any index movements, since they are assumed to have unchanging
  prices, or they are matrix priced which defeats the object of the index.

- There should be consideration of the desirability of publishing indices which are based on, say, three or less securities. If this is caused by the maturity sub-groups ranges, should they be combined?

»Example

In October 1993, the Danish government bond Tracker maturity ranges consisted of the following numbers of bonds:

1-3 years	5 bonds
3-5 years	2 bonds
5-7 years	1 bond
7-10 years	2 bonds
10+ years	1 bond

- Needless to say, it is important to calculate indices only for those areas where adequate tradeable prices are available on a daily basis. Especially in some of the smaller markets, this is not always the case.

Chapter 12

Money/cash market indices

As described earlier, the purpose of a bond index is to emulate the performance of a portfolio which is invested in equal proportions in the issued bonds in the market sector. If no bonds are issued or redeemed in the sector, then the constituents of the index will normally remain unchanged. The basic concepts of money/cash market indices are different, since their purpose is to create a measure of the performance of a fund's cash. The cash may appear or disappear on any day, independently of the performance of the bond market. Some of these cashflows may be connected with the payment of coupons, new issues and redemptions.

As a result, in order to create an objective money market index yardstick, it is assumed that an equal amount of cash is available for investment on every business day and that, on average, the funds are available for investment for a specified time-horizon. Various investment time-horizons were considered.

Although it was decided to invest an equal amount on each business day, an alternative scenario would be to invest an equal amount on each calendar day as, in nearly all money markets, interest accrues on a calendar-day basis. In effect, this would normally mean that three times as much money was available for investment on a Monday as on a Tuesday, Wednesday, Thursday or Friday. This alternative scenario was rejected since,

- it would bias the index to Monday investment rates;

- the cashflows of a fund occur at random dates;

- it would make any adjustments for the fund's actual cashflows difficult to emulate;

- the amount being redeemed might not be equal to the amount being reinvested.

»Example

If cash is invested in 3-month eurodollar deposits, then it can be compared with an index which assumes that $1000 is invested on each business day for 3 months. Each day $1000 worth of investments would be redeemed and would be reinvested in 3-month eurodollars.

Thus the total money market portfolio will consist of around 65 (13 weeks' worth) of $1000 investments. The average life of the index will be close to 1.5 months.

On each day, all the investments (deposits) are valued (i.e. a present value is calculated), based on the available money market rates and the return of the original investments. The indices are derived from the sum of these values.

In most money markets, it is normal for interest rates to be quoted only for specific periods (e.g. overnight, 2 days, 7 days, 1 month, 2 months, 3 months, 6 months and 1 year). The calculations assume that interest rates are calculated for other periods using linear interpolation between the quoted rates, i.e. for a market where m day and n day interest rates, I_m and I_n, are available, then the assumed interest rate for day $(m + r)$ which is less than n is:

$$I_{m+r} = I_m + \frac{r \times (I_n - I_m)}{(n - m)}$$

If an interest rate is required for a time period beyond that of a quoted rate then it is assumed to be the same as the nearest one.

»Example

If the 2-day interest rate was 8.25 per cent, and the 7-day, 8.5 per cent, then the calculated 3-day interest rate would be:

$$8.25 + \frac{1}{5} \times (8.5 - 8.25) = 8.30\%$$

Similarly, the calculated 4-day interest rate would be 8.35 per cent.

The present value $PV(n,m)$ of a unit n day deposit with a life to maturity of m days, is given by:

$$PV(n,m) = \frac{1 + \frac{n}{d} \times i_n}{1 + \frac{m}{d} \times y_m}$$

where,

i_n original interest rate on the n day deposit. (For an 8 per cent rate, $i_n = 0.08$)

y_m current calculated interest rate for an m day deposit. (For an 8 per cent rate, $y_m = 0.08$)

and,

d assumed number of days in a year. This is normally 360 days (e.g. for US dollars and many other currencies) or 365 days (e.g. for Belgium, Canada, Ireland, Italy and sterling).

Please note that this discounts values using simple interest (as is the convention in the money markets) and not compound interest (a bond market convention).

On the first day, a deposit is included in the index $m = n$ and $i_n = y_m$, and so $PV(n,n) = 1$.

Similarly, at redemption, $PV(n,0) = 1 + \frac{n}{d} \times i_n$

i.e., the redemption value is the original value plus the agreed interest.

»Example

A 3-month (91-day) dollar unit deposit was issued with an interest yield of 7 per cent. It now has 60 days to go, for which the quoted yield is 6 per cent.

The present value PV of the deposit is:

$$PV = \frac{1 + \frac{91}{360} \times 0.07}{1 + \frac{60}{360} \times 0.06}$$

$$= 1.0076$$

Cont.

(cont.)

At redemption this deposit will have a value of:

$$PV = 1 + \frac{91}{360} \times 0.07$$

$$= 1.01769$$

It is possible to calculate money market indices for investments in a variety of term deposits. In particular, it is often possible to calculate indices for 1-month, 2-month, 3-month, 6-month and 12-month deposits. In each case, the average outstanding deposit life in the index is about half that of the original investment.

In calculating the indices, one has to bear in mind the following practical considerations:

- As it is assumed that, on each business day, a deposit is redeemed and another one purchased, each index must be for an exact number of weeks, or else the number of separate deposits in the index will change as a result of weekends and bank holidays. Similarly, it is convenient to assume that deposits can be redeemed and purchased on bank holidays. For new deposits, the previous day's rates will be assumed.

  If one does not make these assumptions, it is possible for two deposits—taken out on different days—to be redeemed on the same date.

»Example

30-day deposits would be redeemed as follows:

Day taken out	Redemption day
Monday	Wednesday
Tuesday	Thursday
Wednesday	Friday
Thursday	Monday (32 days)
Friday	Monday (31 days)

An alternative approach is to adjust the deposit life by a day or two, so that one deposit is redeemed on each day.

- The formulae assume that the index is already populated with deposits for each day. At the base date, it is possible to assume that the index is already populated, or that the first deposit is just being invested. This latter assumption means that the performance of the index differs from that of a fully-populated index in its first few months, and so could differ from that of the fund's cash portfolio. As a result, the former option—of a fully-populated index at the base date—is recommended.

The formulae for calculating the price index, total return index and average yield are described below.

Price index

The price index *PI* of a money market index gives the estimated average present value of the deposits, assuming constant deposits of 100. The price index at time *t* is given by:

$$PI_{n,t} = \frac{100}{n_B} \times \sum_{j \varepsilon B} PV_t\,(n,m_j)$$

where,

$PI_{n,t}$	price index of n day deposits at time t
n	length of the original deposits in calendar days
n_B	number of business days in the index
m_j	number of calendar days remaining for the jth deposit
$PV_t\,(n,m_j)$	present value of the jth unit n day deposit at time t, which has a remaining life of m_j days
B	the set of the remaining number of business days for the deposits in the index, (i.e. from 1 to n calendar days)

The summation is over all deposits with the business days in the period (i.e. with a life to maturity of not more than n days).

In the above price index formula,

$$n_B = \sum_{j \varepsilon B} 1$$

Please note the formula gives an index value which does not start at 100.

The present value PV of the deposits at time t are given as before by:

$$PV_t\ (n,m_j) = \frac{1 + \dfrac{n}{d} \times i_n}{1 + \dfrac{m_j}{d} \times y_{mj}}$$

where,

i_n	original interest rate on the jth n day deposit (for an 8 per cent rate, $i_n = 0.08$)
y_{mj}	interest rate for an m_j day deposit (for an 8 per cent rate, $y_{mj} = 0.08$)
d	the assumed number of days in a year. In most markets this is 360 days (e.g. US dollars) or 365 days (e.g. sterling).

Total return index

The total return index TR at time t is given by:

$$TR_{n,0} = 100$$

$$TR_{n,t} = TR_{n,t-1} \times \frac{\displaystyle\sum_{j \varepsilon B} PV_t\ (n,m_j) + i_n^t \times \frac{n}{d}}{\displaystyle\sum_{j \varepsilon B} PV_{t-1}\ (n,m_j)}$$

where,

$TR_{n,t}$	total return index of n day deposits at time t
n	length of the original deposit in calendar days
m_j	number of calendar days remaining for the jth deposit
$PV_t\ (n,m_j)$	present value of the jth unit n day deposit at time t, which has a remaining life of m_j days
B	the set of the remaining number of business days for the deposits in the index, (i.e. from 1 to n calendar days)
i_n^t	original interest rate on the n day deposit which was re-deemed at time t

d   assumed number of days in a year—in most markets this
             is 360 days (e.g. US dollars) or 365 days (e.g. sterling).

The summations are over all business days in the period from 1 day to n
days.

Average yield

The average yield YD for the n day deposits at time t is given by:

$$YD_{n,t} = 100 \times \frac{\sum\limits_{j\varepsilon B} j \times y_{t,mj}}{\sum\limits_{j\varepsilon B} j}$$

where,

$YD_{n,t}$ average yield of n day deposits at time t
n length of the deposit in calendar days
m_j number of calendar days remaining for the jth deposit
$y_{t,mj}$ calculated interest rate for an m_j day deposit at time t
B the set of the remaining number of business days for the
             deposits in the index, (i.e. from 1 to n calendar days).

The summations are over all business days in the period from 1 day to n
days.

It should be noted that the yields are weighted by the outstanding lives
of the deposits in calculating an average life. An interest rate for one month
is obviously much more significant for the total return than one for one
day. This is similar to the average gross redemption yield calculations for
the bond indices where the values are weighted by the duration of the
bonds.

Such calculations can be easily applied to deposits, certificates of deposit
and commercial paper which may be issued on any day. The formulae can
easily be modified to apply to Treasury bills as well, which are issued at
regular, but not daily, intervals. However, in this latter case, the average life
of the index will oscillate over time.

Chapter 13
Published indices

In addition to the Bloomberg/EFFAS government bond indices, Datastream and the ISMA have committed to calculating indices according to the revised EFFAS methodology and formulae. However, as would be expected, there are some differences in the implementations for different markets.

Bloomberg/EFFAS government bond indices

Type of security: Domestic government bonds for:
                       Australia, Austria, Belgium, Canada, Denmark, Finland, France, Germany, Ireland, Italy, Japan, Netherlands, New Zealand, Norway, Portugal, Spain, Sweden, United Kingdom and United States

Type of index: All-bond
                       Tracker (Q2 1994)
                       Bellwether (Q2 1994)

Maturity bands: All
                       1-3 years
                       3-5 years
                       5-7 years
                       7-10 years
                       10+ years

Base date: 31 December 1991

Where published: On the Bloomberg system

Datastream government bond indices

Type of security: Domestic government bonds for:
                       Australia, Austria, Belgium, Canada, Denmark, France, Germany, Ireland, Italy, Japan,
Cont.

	(cont.) Netherlands, Spain, Sweden, Switzerland, United Kingdom and United States (May be extended to other areas in the future)
Type of index:	All-bond (Q1 1994) Tracker (Q2 1994) Bellwether (Q2 1994)
Maturity bands:	All 1-3 years 3-5 years 5-7 years 7-10 years 10+ years Irredeemables (UK only)
Base date:	30 December 1988, although planning to calculate the history further back for some markets
Where published:	On the Datastream system — Publication in the Financial Times expected

ISMA eurobond indices

Type of security:	Eurobonds in the following currencies: Australian dollar, Canadian dollar, Deutschemark, European currency unit, French franc, Italian lira, Japanese yen, Luxembourg franc, New Zealand dollar, Portuguese escudo, Spanish peseta, sterling, Swiss franc and US dollar
Type of index:	Tracker only
Maturity bands:	All 1-5 years 5+ years
Base date:	31 December 1990
Other criteria:	The selection only consists of those non callable securities for which the ISMA receives

adequate prices. An adequate price is defined in terms of the minimum number of market-makers and the maximum acceptable price spread

Where published: In the *Weekly Eurobond Guide* (an ISMA publication). Available in electronic form on a daily basis to ISMA members and information providers, including Bloomberg, Datastream and Reuters

Chapter 14

Summary of bond index construction rules

The following summarizes the principal conclusions for standardized rules in the construction and calculation of bond indices.

Formulae

- Chain-linked   - to allow for change
- Arithmetical   - to emulate a portfolio
- Cashflows   - reinvested in the index
- Bond selection   - reviewed each month

Market coverage

Three possible types of index

- All-bond   - often only available for government securities
- Tracker   - most appropriate for all professional investors
- Bellwether   - most liquid bonds

Maturity sub-groups

Based on expected 'operative' life, not duration. Suggested maturity sub-groups have operative lives at the beginning of the selection period of:

- 1-3 years
- 3-5 years
- 5-7 years
- 7-10 years
- Over 10 years
- Irredeemables

In some markets, these may be grouped into larger maturity bands, e.g. 1-5 years and over 5 years.

Special calculations are used for securities with a final maturity of less than 1 year (*see* Chapter 12, 'Money/cash market indices').

Bond types included

'Normal' fixed-rate bonds with predictable cashflows. Indices using the same formulae can be created for other homogenous sub-groups. e.g.:

- Index-linked bonds   - based on the same index (e.g. UK government index-linked bonds).
- Floating-rate notes   - the price and total return index calculations will be comparable, although the other calculations may not be.

Range of calculations

- Clean price index
- Gross price index
- Total return index
- Interest paid this year
- Average coupon
- Average life
- Average duration
- Average convexity
- Average redemption yield
- Average current yield

Prices used

- Closing mid-prices

Settlement date

This is required for the accrued interest and yield calculations. Normal dates for the market. For example:

- 2 business days for Bundesrepublik issues
- 3 business days for Italian government bonds.
  or,
- currently, 7 calendar days for eurobonds and Dutch securities.

Accrual basis

As used in the primary market of the security.

Chapter 15

The future

The methodology suggested in the previous chapters can be extended in a variety of areas.

In particular we have concentrated on the domestic government bond markets or on all bonds in a market. Each market could be subdivided into a number of sectorial groups. Possible industry sectors that may be appropriate in some markets are:

- Domestic government/public sector bonds
    Government
    Government-guaranteed
    Agency
    Local authority
    Mortgage institutions
    Other

- Domestic corporate bonds
    Industrial
    Utility
    Banks
    Other finance
    Other

- Foreign bonds
    Government and government-guaranteed
    Supranational
    Other

- Eurobonds
    Government and government-guaranteed
    Supranational
    Other

Additionally, it is expected that special indices could in future be calculated for the following categories of bonds. For these categories, the calculations for the clean price and the total return indices will be similar to those described, however the average index values may be different.

»Bond Feature

Index-linked bonds	For those indexed to an inflation measure, real returns may be calculated
Floating-rate notes	Could calculate average discounted margins
Convertibles into equities	Need to know how much has been converted at each date
Special taxation groups	
Mortgage or asset-backed securities	Assumptions have to be made about the expected average redemption date

---

Another approach might be to subdivide bonds according to the expectation of their durations, or even to calculate indices based on constant average life or duration. As described earlier, this latter proposal does not in fact emulate the performance of the market and will probably require a different methodological basis.

Another area where future investigation is desirable is that of constructing global indices from a variety of local market indices.

All of the global market indices which are widely reported are currently constructed by weighting together the local market indices according to the local bond market capitalization. Although this has become the norm, there are a number of alternative scenarios which could be considered.

If one weights together local markets according to their capitalization a number of problems can occur.

- The markets may have different liquidity.

- Some bond markets may be large, due to limited control in the past over inflation.

- New issues, rather than the value of outstanding stocks, will often be more important in influencing liquidity.

- What is the boundary between the money and bond markets?

In most markets, this boundary is assumed to be one year but, as already been mentioned, French BTAN issues with a life of up to 5 years were considered money market instruments.

- What is the boundary between the 'cash' market and the derivatives market?

Alternative approaches involve weighting the local indices by the gross domestic products of the markets they represent, using the OECD Purchasing Power Parity (PPP) exchange rate to convert the values to US dollars, or looking at the size of the country's world trade.

These approaches are discussed in some detail in the article 'Towards a European Bond Index' by Paul Temperton in the *European Bond Markets*, 5th Edition (*see* Bibliography).

Chapter 16

Bibliography

- *Datastream/EFFAS Bond Indices - A Review*, Koos't Hart and Peter van der Linde, August 1990

- *European Bond Markets, The*, Stuart K. McLean - Editor, 5th Edition, November 1992

- *Formulae for Yield and Other Calculations* - 2nd Edition (ISMA), Patrick Brown, January 1992

- *FT-Actuaries British Government Securities Indices, The*, Journal of the Institute of Actuaries - Volume 106, A.D. Wilkie, 1978

- *FT-Actuaries British Government Securities Indices, The*, Journal of the Institute of Actuaries - Volume 107 III, A.D. Wilkie, 1979

- *Guide to European Domestic Bond Markets*, 3rd Edition, September 1986. The Datastream/EFFAS European Domestic Bond Indices, Patrick Brown

- *J.P. Morgan Government Bond Index*, Victor Filatov - 2nd Edition, December 1990

- *J.P. Morgan Ecu Bond Index*, Peter Crawford, June 1991

- *J.P. Morgan Cash Index, Introducing The*, December 1990

- *J.P. Morgan Cash Index, Replicating The*, John N Lobley and Kevin M. Murphy, March 1991

- *Normes Applicables au Marché Obligataire Domestique Francais*, Comité de Normalisation Obligataire, June 1992

Cont.

(cont.)

- *Rachats en Bourse,* Revue des Actuaires de Paris, Albert Allanic, March 1975

- *Rex - German Bond Index,* Frankfurter Wertpapierbörse, Frank Mella, June 1991

- *Salomon Brothers World Government Bond Index, Expansion & Definition,* July 1992

- *Salomon Brothers Eurodollar Bond Index, Introducing the New,* January 1994

Appendix A

Geometric indices

Indices have been published in various financial markets, using both geometric and arithmetical calculations. Geometric calculations are used for indices such as the Financial Times 30 Equity Index, and the Dow Jones Industrial Average index. The basic principle used in the calculation is to multiply the prices of all the n constituents together, take the nth root, and then multiply by a factor to produce the index. When the constituents of the index are changed, the factor is adjusted, so that there is no discontinuity in the values. Although this approach is reasonably good at reflecting price movements over a short time period, it is easy to show that it does not reflect the performance of a portfolio.

»Example

Consider a portfolio of two securities A and B. The holding for both securities is $1,000,000 of nominal value and they both priced at 100 per cent at the beginning of the period, being evaluated.

Thus, the initial value of the portfolio is:

$$1,000,000 \times \frac{100}{100} + 1,000,000 \times \frac{100}{100} = \$2,000,000$$

If the price of security A doubles to 200 per cent, whereas that of security B halves to 50 per cent, then the value of the portfolio is now:

$$1,000,000 \times \frac{200}{100} + 1,000,000 \times \frac{50}{100} = \$2,500,000$$

Hence the value of the portfolio has increased by 25 per cent over the period, and so an equivalent index should also rise by 25 per cent in the period.

Cont.

(cont.)

Let us assume that there is a geometrically-calculated index which consists of the same two securities. The value of this index at beginning of the period will be:

$$\text{Factor} \times (100 \times 100)^{0.5} = \text{Factor} \times 100$$

At the end of the period it will be:

$$\text{Factor} \times (200 \times 50)^{0.5} = \text{Factor} \times 100$$

It has not changed over the period, and so does not reflect the performance of an equivalent portfolio.

Another problem with geometrically-constructed indices is that they do not reflect the relative size of the constituents. All the constituents are assumed to have an equal weight. This is valid if the universe of bonds is very large, and one is comparing the performance of a very small portfolio with it. However, if the portfolio has a reasonable part of the universe, this approach must be challenged.

As a result, geometrically-calculated bond indices were rejected in favour of arithmetically-calculated ones which more closely reflect the performance of a portfolio.

Appendix B
Members of the bond index sub-committee

Stuart McLean
Euromoney EXPOs
(Chairman)

Patrick J. Brown
International Securities Market Association
(Secretary)

Stuart Bell
Bloomberg L.P.

Adrian Carr
J.P. Morgan Securities

Francesca Edwards
J.P. Morgan Securities

Christopher Golden
Lehman Brothers International

Jean Granoux
Comité de Normalisation Obligataire

Koos't Hart
Mees Pierson Capital Management

Nicholas Howard
J.P. Morgan Securities

Richard Komarnicki
Diagram France

Cont.

(cont.)

Peter Lockyer
Clay & Partners

Carsten Mahler
Danske Invest

Richard Pagan
Salomon Brothers International

Andrew Sabourin
Datastream International

Peter Schedling
Oesterreichische Kontrollbank

David Self
International Securities Market Association

Charles Taylor
Bloomberg L.P.

Paul Temperton
The Independent Economic Research Company Ltd.

Robert Tyley
Paribas Limited

Peter van der Linde
Philips Pensionenfondsen

Index